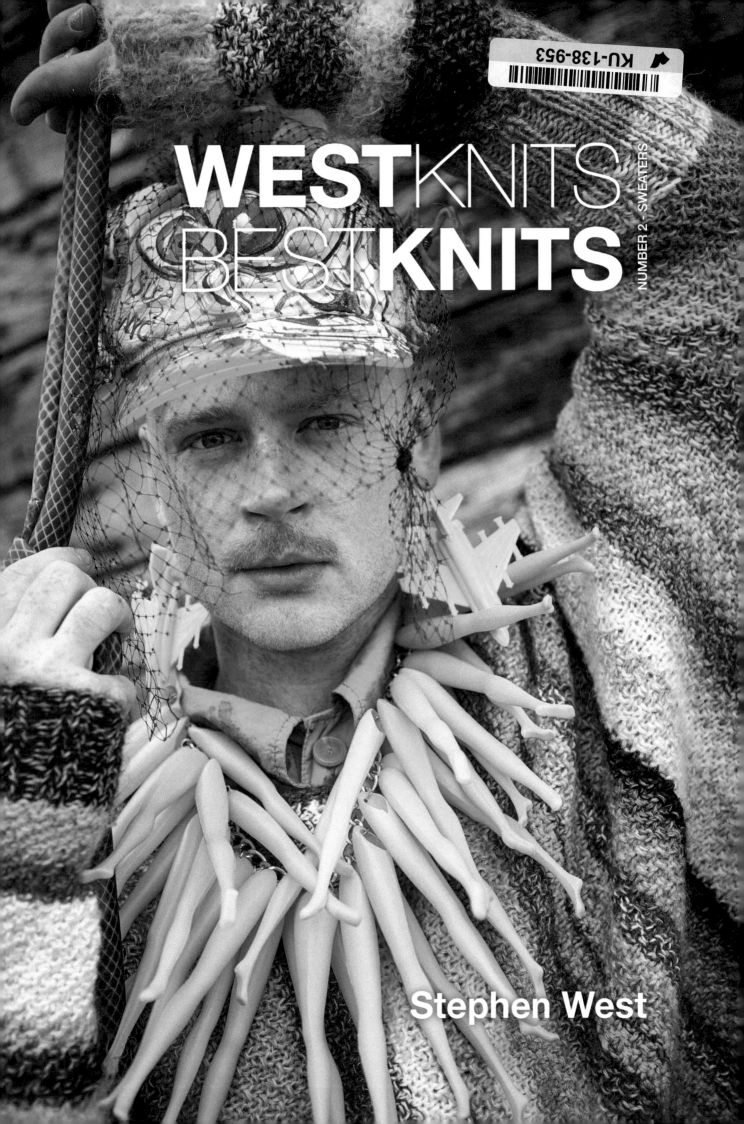

WESTKNITS
BESTKNITS

NUMBER 2 - SWEATERS

Stephen West

Patterns and Instructions
STEPHEN WEST

Page Layout and Book Design
NANCY MARCHANT

West, Stephen, 1988-
Westknits Bestknits: Number 2 - Sweaters
172 pages
ISBN/EAN: 978-0-9851317-7-7

FIRST EUROPEAN EDITION

CONTENTS

STEPHEN WEST

The first sweater I ever knit was a textured pullover with simple cable motifs and set-in sleeves during my first year of college. I remember knitters warning me about sweaters and how long they take to knit. Some knitters told me it took six months to knit a sweater. Despite those warnings, I started a blue sweater with an alpaca/wool blend and finished within two weeks. Those sweater warnings clearly did not properly estimate my obsession with knitting all day every day. I was proud that my blue sweater actually fit, but I soon discovered that would not be a regular occurrence. I learned about gauge by making several ill-fitted garments. Thank goodness for felting and aggressive blocking!

Many of my early sweater experiments resulted from reading books by Elizabeth Zimmermann. She encouraged me to follow my own rules using a pattern as a guideline. I also learned a lot about sweater construction by modifying existing patterns. My favorite patterns were written for women with bust and waist shaping so I re-worked several designs and lengthened them to fit my proportions. I used to the think that being a "good knitter" meant mastering skills like lace, intarsia, and fair isle while achieving tailored fitted garments. Those were the types of respected patterns I saw in most Ravelry patterns and print publications. I learned through the years that I preferred simple stitch patterns while playing with color and shape. I became more interested in creating my own styles instead of reproducing traditional sweater constructions. What if a sweater doesn't always have to be top-down or bottom-up?

Many of the sweaters in this book are knit up, down, and all around. This multi-directional or modular approach is often a result of not knowing what I'm knitting when I begin. I usually start with a palette of colors and a fascination like a particular stitch pattern or shape. I follow my fascinations and let the colors and my mood guide me. I like to use my favorite colors first because I believe if I'm passionate with the first section of a project, it inspires me to continue with vigor. When I'm unsure about a color combination, I rarely rip out my knitting. I either don't use that color again or I add ten more colors and that usually solves all color concerns.

Soon after I learned brioche knitting from Nancy Marchant in 2014, I cast on for a hat, but I continued increasing because I loved knitting brioche so much. My hat soon became a sweater and I was in love, but it wasn't enough. I still had a big pile of beautiful yarns in front of me so I kept knitting until I produced an Askews Me Dress. This accidental dress delighted me because I never planned to make it.

The Askews Me Poncho begins with the same cowl neck and yoke increases as the Askews Me Sweater & Dress. Instead of dividing for the body and sleeves, continue knitting the three increases as they spiral into a wide drapey poncho. Working two-color brioche in the round is much easier than working flat brioche because you always knit the foreground color (black) and purl the background color (white). When knitting a project with only two colors, make sure the yarns are extra soft and special. Woolfolk Får merino wool is the softest wool I've ever felt and it produces the squishiest brioche fabric. You will never want to take off this plush brioche poncho.

I attempted to make a brioche hat using darker yarns after knitting the Askews Me Dress. Again, I couldn't stop knitting as more colors flew onto my needles and eventually my hat became a moody Askews Me Sweater. This sweater is the same pattern as the Askews Me Dress except you bind off earlier and add long sleeves. I love pairing neutrals with color pops in brioche knitting because you get dramatic highlights or shadows in the fabric. Combining saturated colors on the front with solid black on the back deepens the entire palette and helps tone down vibrant colors. I prefer to improvise my color choices as I knit. When I run out of yarn, it's an opportunity to use another color!

The Amazing Technicolor Dream Sweater began by knitting a marled legwarmer at my friend Ragga's house in Iceland. She walked by and tried it on her arm and said it would make a great sleeve. I didn't bring a sweater's quantity of yarn with me so I dove into Ragga's yarn stash and mixed all of her colorful fingering and lace weight yarns together to knit the oversized sideways constructed sweater. I used a variety of hand dyed superwash wools combined with Icelandic wool naturally dyed by Guðrún Bjarnadóttir. I found that including woolly non-superwash wools and fluffy mohair helped to create a lofty garment with more structure. You can still see the glimpse of a leg warmer with ribbing in the middle of the left sleeve. I rarely rip back in my knitting or in life. Instead, I incorporate and embrace variations in the design process.

Watch Your Back is a thicker version of my popular Eyeball Shawl pattern. I adjusted the increases and created a large and in charge super eye and a small version for my Icelandic mini me, Karítas. Karítas is an expert dance mover and groover and totally represents the Westknits spirit in Reykjavík.

Watch Your Back comes in a super squishy worsted weight gauge. You can wrap it around for a cozy scarf or drape it over your shoulders for the cutest eyeball shrug. No knitted eye is complete without coordinating Barbie arms and legs necklaces!

Penguno began by casting on a rectangle and knitting seed stitch one evening until I was tired. I woke up the next day and decided I had the back of a mystery garment. I picked up along one edge, knitted a few welts and continued working sideways until the fabric wrapped around my body. The remaining process was a matter of solving a puzzle and figuring out how to seamlessly piece all the sections together. I became obsessed with the chunky construction and finished my first sample in five days! When I tried it on upside down, I was completely surprised by the longer silhouette.

Penguono can be sporty by day with short sleeves or dramatically elegant in the evening when you wear it upside down. If you knit a Penguono, you are officially part of the Penguono Posse, a collection of fearless international knitters obsessed with fiber, color, and style.

Enchanted Mesa began with a short row asymmetrical yoke inspired by my Dotted Rays shawl. I love how short rows create an organic flowing fabric. There are many popular methods like the wrap & turn or German short row method, but I use the Westknits Shortcut Row. You simply stop your row, turn around, and go! There are no slips or wraps required. After completing all the turns, I usually decorate each short row gap with a big yarn over hole. Enchanted Mesa is designed to use a mixed assortment of yarn types.

Don't be afraid to combine angora, wool, alpaca, and mohair yarns. Feel free to vary your yarn weights as well. Many Westknits sweaters written for worsted weight yarn also incorporate DK and aran weight yarns. Use the needle size you like with the thickest yarn weight and any finer yarns will just have a lighter drape with a thinner density.

When I work on large garter stitch projects like Parachutey, I like to keep the shaping simple and mindless so I can enjoy the colorful stripes and soft yarns. The sideways construction of the front piece yields super flattering stripes. I rarely pre-plan the color layout. I start with my favorite color/s and improvise while playing with a range of thick and thin stripes. When I'm working with several bold color pops I almost always mix in a heavy dose of neutrals like white and gray. The back is knit top-down with I-cord bind offs finishing the edges of this boxy shape. I originally intended to pick up and add sleeves for an oversized t-shirt. Once I tried it on, I was pleasantly surprised with this tank top silhouette and called it complete.

Marled Magic was inspired by my Marled Magic Mystery Shawl KAL in 2017. The sweater begins with the first four sections of the Marled Magic Shawl. I draped those first four sections on my body to determine where I wanted it to drape. Then, I picked up to knit more sections across one half of my body and mirrored those shapes with different textures on the other half. These modular constructions are a fun puzzle to solve. When I'm unfamiliar with the final destination, I make sure to keep the stitch patterns simple while working with colors that make me squirm with delight.

Marled Magic uses two strands of fingering or lace weight yarns held together throughout the entire project. I chose to include several colors of mohair to keep the fabric light and flowy. When working with marled patterns like Marled Magic and Amazing Technicolor Dream Sweater, start with a plentiful palette of colors and textures. More is more and less is a bore with these multi-colored sweaters. Mix neutrals together with color pops to provide a sense of breath and space throughout the fabric. If a color doesn't work, add ten more colors! I often use a balanced palette of light, medium, and dark colors to provide contrast possibilities. A little bit of dark gray or black can go a long way and help the other colors pop out.

I focus on color first and yarn type second. If a certain texture or yarn base bothers you, either simplify your yarn selection or introduce two or three other types of textures like tweed or fuzzy fibers into your palette. Mohair can completely transform your fabric. I prefer lace weight mohair/silk blends held together with fingering weight wools to add a fuzzy soft filter to all the colors. Just one or two balls of mohair/silk adds vast dimension to a project. I'm constantly surprised how wildly colorful yarns become more subtle when held together with mohair. Textured yarns and color pops are like spicy ingredients. They can pack a big punch knit on their own, but if you use them in smaller doses or mixed with neutrals, they produce more sophisticated variations.

Kangarullover has a long history. I originally started this design three years before publishing this book. The first attempt was made with rustic wool, but I didn't write the pattern down so I made a second chunky version while writing the pattern. I still didn't complete the pattern so I made a third sample using black and white with a golden yellow accent. I do not recommend this multiple sample method of pattern writing, but thankfully I have a lot of yarn and love to knit so I don't mind re-knitting colorful garments. After writing the pattern, I desperately wanted a splashy speckled pullover. My friend and fellow speckle addict, Chantal, knitted one

for me in a smaller size. Chantal's color sense is crazy on point and she is a strong believer in spicing up any project with more yellow. One speckled Kangarullover with fun fur and sparkly accents was not enough so I created coordinating shorts called Kangarorts to match! Finally, my Kangarullover dreams came true with bonus big boy baggy britches!

I hope you find a world of inspiration and fearless color combinations within this Westknits collection. I encourage you to use these patterns as guidelines to create your own unique creations. Follow your color instincts and let your imagination run wild!

AMAZING
TECHNICOLOR
DREAM
SWEATER

AMAZING TECHNICOLOR DREAM SWEATER

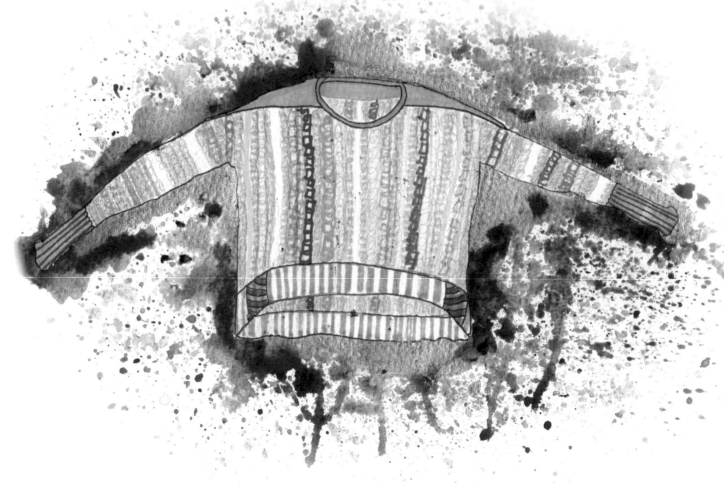

Dive into your stash and gather an array of colorful fingering weight yarns for this sideways constructed pullover. The colorful journey begins with the sleeves and textural moss stitch. Hold two strands of yarn together throughout the entire project for a melty marled effect. The two front halves are joined in the center with a visible seam. A simple back rectangle provides another canvas for colorful stripes. The shoulders are worked in garter stitch while seamlessly attaching to the front and back pieces. Short rows raise the back neck and an I-cord bind off finishes the v-neckline. Decreases shape the bottom front edge for a subtle sloped effect. Choose to leave your striped ends as fringe or pick up along the bottom edge to knit an optional two-color brioche border.

Sizes: Small [Medium, Large]
Medium size is shown on a 41" / 104cm chest circumference with approximately 27" / 69cm of positive ease.
Measurements are written in the pattern for sleeve length and the distance to knit the sideways front and back pieces. Instructions also include landmarks on the body so you can achieve proportions that work for you.

For example, "Work even until sleeve reaches approximately 1" / 2.5cm past your elbow."

Finished Measurements: 60 [68, 68]" / 152 [173, 173]cm chest circumference, 18.5 [21, 22.5]" / 47 [53, 57]cm front length measured from top of shoulder by neck edge. Measurements taken after blocking.

Yarn: Fingering weight held double. Worsted weight yarns can be substituted if you hold one single strand.

To get a blended ombre effect in sections of the fabric, arrange colors from light to dark. For example...

Work Color A & Color B together. Break A.
Work Color B & Color C together. Break B.
Work Color C & Color D together. Break C.

To get sharper contrasting stripes, break both strands of yarn and replace them with 2 new strands.

Yardage: Approximately 2200 [2500, 2700] yds / 2012 [2286, 2469]m total of fingering weight yarn. If you choose to substitute worsted weight yarn held single you will need approximately 1100 [1250, 1400]yds / 1006 [1143, 1280]m total

The shoulders and collar require approximately 100 [120, 120]yds / 91 [110,110]m. The sample used a single strand of worsted weight yarn for the garter stitch shoulders and collar.

Shown in: A variety of fingering weight stash yarns including wool, alpaca, and mohair blends. Hand dyed speckled colors blend beautifully for the marled blending. Samples include fingering weight yarns from Walk Collection, Hedgehog Fibres, Madelinetosh, Woolfolk, Qing Fibre, and worsted weight cormo wool from Hello Mello Handspun.

Needles: 40" US 8 / 5mm circular

Notions: 1 stitch marker, tapestry needle

Gauge: 18 sts & 28 rows = 4" / 10cm in moss stitch

Pattern Notes: Instructions are written assuming the knitter knows how to work with a 2-stitch repeat (moss stitch) while shaping (increasing and decreasing).

INSTRUCTIONS

RIGHT SLEEVE

CO 36 [40, 44] sts. Place marker and join to work in the rnd.

(K2, p2) to end of rnd.

Repeat 2x2 ribbing until ribbing reaches your desired length. The cuff from the sample with fringe measures approximately 2.5" / 6cm. The sample with blue cuffs measures approximately 9" / 23cm. If you would like to add a thumbhole, work 2" / 5cm of ribbing in the rnd and then work the ribbing flat for 3" / 8cm to create a vertical thumb opening before joining the cuff in the rnd again. Continue with Moss Stitch pattern once you're finished with the ribbed cuff.

MOSS STITCH

Rnds 1 & 2: (K1, p1) to end of rnd.
Rnds 3 & 4: (P1, k1) to end of rnd.

Work moss stitch while increasing at the beginning and end of every 6th [8th, 8th] rnd until you reach 50 [54, 58] sts.
For example, during an increase rnd, M1L, work all sts in moss stitch, M1R. Feel free to substitute and select your favorite increase method and work one increase before the first stitch and another increase after the last stitch. You will have 2 extra sts after each increase rnd.

Work even until sleeve measures approximately 15 [17, 17]" / 38 [43, 43]cm from CO edge or until sleeve reaches approximately 1" / 2.5cm past your elbow.

RIGHT FRONT

CO 56 [66, 70] sts using the cable CO method,

Next Row (RS): K1, work the remaining 55 [65, 69] stitches in moss stitch followed by the next 24 [26, 28] sleeve stitches in moss stitch, sl1 wyif. Slip the remaining 25 [27, 29] sleeve stitches onto waste yarn or a stitch holder.
Next Row (WS): K1, work in moss stitch to the last 3 sts, k2tog, sl1 wyif.

Row 1 (RS): K1, work in moss stitch to last st, sl1 wyif.
Row 2 (WS): K1, work in moss stitch to last 3 sts, k2tog, sl1 wyif.

Repeat last 2 rows 12 more times. 67 [79, 85] sts remain.

Work back and forth in moss stitch (without decreases) while always knitting the first stitch and slipping the last stitch wyif in every row. Continue knitting until work measures approximately 10 [12, 12]" / 25 [30, 30]cm from cable CO edge or knit until work reaches the right edge of your neck.

Next Row (RS): K1, work in moss stitch to last st, sl1 wyif.
Next Row (WS): K1, ssk, work in moss stitch to last st, sl1 wyif.

Repeat last 2 rows 12 more times. 54 [66, 72] sts remain. BO all sts on the next RS row.

LEFT SLEEVE

Create left sleeve using the same Right Sleeve instructions.

LEFT FRONT

BO 25 [27, 29] sts. Work the remaining 25 [27, 29] sts in moss stitch, CO 56 [66, 70] sts using the cable CO method. Turn to work WS.

Next Row (WS): K1, ssk, work 53 [63, 67] sts in moss stitch followed by the next 24 [26, 28] sleeve stitches in moss stitch, sl1 wyif. 80 [92, 98] sts total.

Row 1 (RS): K1, work in moss stitch to last st, sl1 wyif.
Row 2 (WS): K1, ssk, work in moss stitch to last st, sl1 wyif.

Repeat last two rows 12 more times. 67 [79, 85] sts remain.

Work back and forth in moss stitch (without decreases) while always knitting the first stitch and slipping the last stitch wyif in every row. Continue knitting until work measures approximately 10 [12, 12]" / 25 [30, 30]cm from cable CO edge or knit until work reaches the left edge of your neck.

Next Row (RS): K1, work in moss stitch to last st, sl1 wyif.
Next Row (WS): K1, work in moss stitch to last 3 sts, k2tog, sl1 wyif.

Repeat last 2 rows 12 more times. 54 [66, 72] sts remain. BO all sts on the next RS row.

Seam Right Front BO edge together to Left Front BO edge. The photographed sample has a seam that is visible on the RS. You can choose to feature the seam or hide it on the WS of the fabric.

BACK
Place 25 [27, 29] right sleeve sts from waste yarn onto needle. With RS facing, k1, work 24 [26, 28] sts in moss stitch, pick up and k56 [66, 70] sts along the cable CO edge from the right front. 81 [93, 99] total sts.

Next Row (WS): K1, work in moss stitch to last st, sl1 wyif.

Work back and forth in moss stitch (without decreases) while always knitting the first stitch and slipping the last stitch wyif in every row. Continue knitting until work reaches the left sleeve sts that were bound off. You should have the same number of rows across the back as the right and left fronts added together.
BO all sts on the next RS row. Seam the back to the left sleeve and left side edge.

LEFT SHOULDER
Follow this link for a video tutorial on the shoulder technique.
http://youtu.be/v5Zaqe4s2OE

Shoulder instructions are written using color C. You can use any color for the shoulders and neckline. I recommend a single strand of worsted weight wool to provide more structure to the shoulders.

Using color C and starting at the opening where the FRONT and BACK separate from the LEFT SLEEVE , pick up and k2 sts in the gap between the FRONT and BACK. Turn to work WS.

Next Row (WS): K1, ssk (next st together with a picked up selvedge st from the BACK edge).
Next Row (RS): Sl1 wyif then place the yarn in back to knit, M1L, sl1 wyif, pick up a selvedge stitch from the FRONT edge and slip it onto right needle.
Next Row (WS): K2tog (the picked up selvedge stitch together with the slipped color C stitch), kfb, ssk (next st together with a picked up selvedge st from the BACK edge).

Row 1 (RS): Sl1 wyif then place the yarn in back to knit, k to last st, sl1 wyif, pick up a selvedge stitch from the FRONT edge and slip it onto right needle.
Row 2 (WS): K2tog (the picked up selvedge stitch together with the slipped color C stitch), k to last st, ssk (next st together with a picked up selvedge st from the BACK edge).

Repeat last 2 rows twice more.

The first time you work Row 7, you can ignore "k to last 2 sts" and proceed immediately to "kfb, sl1wyif..." since there are only 4 total sts.

Row 7 (RS): Sl1 wyif then place the yarn in back to knit, kfb, k to last 2 sts, kfb, sl1 wyif, pick up a selvedge stitch from the FRONT edge and slip it onto right needle.
Row 8 (WS): K2tog (the picked up selvedge stitch together with the slipped color C stitch), k to last st, ssk (next st together with a picked up selvedge st from the BACK edge).

Repeat last 8 rows until you reach the the beginning of the FRONT neck shaping, ending with a WS row. Break yarn and place sts onto waste yarn or a stitch holder.

RIGHT SHOULDER

Using color C and starting at the opening where the FRONT and BACK separate from the RIGHT SLEEVE , pick up and k2 sts in the gap between the FRONT and BACK. Turn to work WS.

Next Row (WS): K1, ssk (next st together with a picked up selvedge st from the FRONT edge).
Next Row (RS): Sl1 wyif then place the yarn in back to knit, M1L, sl1 wyif, pick up a selvedge stitch from the BACK edge and slip it onto right needle.
Next Row (WS): K2tog (the picked up selvedge stitch together with the slipped color C stitch), kfb, ssk (next st together with a picked up selvedge st from the FRONT edge).

Row 1 (RS): Sl1 wyif then place the yarn in back to knit, k to last st, sl1 wyif, pick up a selvedge stitch from the BACK edge and slip it onto right needle.
Row 2 (WS): K2tog (the picked up selvedge stitch together with the slipped color C stitch), k to last st, ssk (next st together with a picked up selvedge st from the FRONT edge).

Repeat last 2 rows twice more.

The first time you work Row 7, you can ignore "k to last 2 sts" and proceed immediately to "kfb, sl1wyif..." since there are only 4 total sts.

Row 7 (RS): Sl1 wyif then place the yarn in back to knit, kfb, k to last 2 sts, kfb, sl1 wyif, pick up a selvedge stitch from the BACK edge and slip it onto right needle.
Row 8 (WS): K2tog (the picked up selvedge stitch together with the slipped color C stitch), k to last st, ssk (next st together with a picked up selvedge st from the FRONT edge).

Repeat last 8 rows until you reach the the

beginning of the FRONT neck shaping, ending with a WS row.

COLLAR

K all RIGHT SHOULDER sts, pick up and k1 st into each selvedge st from BACK, k all LEFT SHOULDER sts, pick up and k1 st into each selvedge st from FRONT v-neck. Place marker and join to work in the rnd.

Next Rnd: P all sts.

SHORT ROWS
Row 1 (RS): K all RIGHT SHOULDER, BACK, and LEFT SHOULDER sts, turn to work WS.
Row 2 (WS): K to 2 sts before beginning of rnd, turn to work RS.

Row 3 (RS): K to 2 sts before last turn, turn to work WS.
Row 4 (WS): K to 2 sts before last turn, turn to work RS.

Repeat last 2 rows until the last short row turn brings you to the corner of the last shoulder stitch and back stitch. For example, if you have 26 shoulder stitches on each shoulder, work a total of 13 short rows back and forth (13 garter ridges).

Next Row (RS): K to end of rnd while closing the short row gaps.
Next Rnd: P to end of rnd while closing the short row gaps.

Next Rnd: (K4, k2tog) across RIGHT SHOULDER, BACK, and LEFT SHOULDER, k across v-neck without decreases to end of rnd.

BO all sts on the next rnd using an I-cord BO as follows, CO 3 sts using the cable CO method, *k2, k2tog tbl, slip 3 sts back to left needle, repeat from * until all sts are bound off. Three I-cord sts remain. Break yarn and pull strand through the remaining 3 sts.

Continue with the optional brioche border or skip to FINISHING instructions.

BRIOCHE BORDER (optional)

This border is written using MC (main color for the foreground) and CC (contrast color for the background). Each rnd is worked twice, first with the MC and again with the CC. The border requires approximately 50g of each color using worsted weight wool.

Set Up Rnd: Using MC and with RS facing, pick up and k15 sts along the right diagonal decrease edge from the RIGHT FRONT, pm, pick up and k1 stitch for each selvedge stitch along the bottom front edge until you reach the LEFT FRONT diagonal edge (this stitch count should be an uneven number for the front pick up), pm, pick up and k15 sts along the left diagonal decrease edge, pm, pick up and k1 stitch for each selvedge stitch along BACK edge (this stitch count should be an uneven number for the back pick up), pm to mark beginning of the rnd.

Set Up Rnd: Using CC, (sl1yo, p1) 7 times, sl1yo, slm, p1, (sl1yo, p1) to m, slm, (sl1yo, p1) 7 times, sl1yo, slm, p1, (sl1yo, p1) to m, slm.

Rnd 1 MC: Using MC, brkyobrk, sl1yo, (brk1, sl1yo) 5 times, brRsldec, slm, sl1yo, (brk1, sl1yo) to m, slm, brLsldec, sl1yo, (brk1, sl1yo) 5 times, brkyobrk, slm, sl1yo, (brk1, sl1yo) to m, slm.

Rnd 1 CC: Using CC, sl1yo, p1, sl1yo, (brp1, sl1yo) 6 times, slm, brp1, (sl1yo, brp1) to m, slm, (sl1yo, brp1) 6 times, sl1yo, p1, sl1yo, slm, brp1, (sl1yo, brp1) to m, slm.

Rnd 2 MC: Using MC, brk1, (sl1yo, brk1) 7 times, slm, sl1yo, (brk1, sl1yo) to m, slm, brk1, (sl1yo, brk1) 7 times, slm, sl1yo, (brk1, sl1yo) to m, slm.

Rnd 2 CC: Using CC, sl1yo, (brp1, sl1yo) 7 times, slm, brp1, (sl1yo, brp1) to m, slm, (sl1yo, brp1) 7 times, sl1yo, slm, brp1, (sl1yo, brp1) to m, slm.

Repeat Rnds 1 & 2 using MC & CC 8 more times or until border reaches your desired length. Break CC.

Next Rnd MC: Using MC, brk1, (k1, brk1) 7 times, slm, k1, (brk1, k1) to m, slm, brk1, (k1, brk1) 7 times, slm, k1, (brk1, k1) to m, slm.

I-cord BO: Cast on 3 sts using the cable cast on method, *k2, k2tog tbl, slip 3 sts onto left needle, repeat from * until all sts are bound off. Break yarn and pull it through the remaining 3 sts.

FINISHING
Weave in ends or leave ends hanging for decorative fringe. Block sweater to smooth the fabric.

ENCHANTED
MESA

ENCHANTED MESA

This top down sweater is a playful canvas for mixing different fibers and yarn weights. Begin at the neckline and knit short rows for an asymmetrical yoke. Continue experimenting with stripes and textures for the body of the sweater. Enchanted Mesa is for adventurous knitters who like to make spontaneous improvisational yarn and color choices. Grab your favorite yarns and have fun!

Sizes: One size, customizable with different gauges.

The pattern is written in one size with DK/Worsted weight yarn (4.5 sts = 1" / 2.5cm). For varying sizes, follow the gauge chart. Swatch with different yarns and needle sizes to get gauge for your desired size. This sweater is meant to fit with a few inches or more of positive ease to accentuate the drape in the body of the sweater. Samples are shown on a 41" / 104cm chest circumference with 2" / 5cm of positive ease and 4.5 sts per inch.

See chart below.

Body and sleeve lengths are customizable.

Yarn: Samples use DK and worsted weight yarns. Try holding fingering weight yarn double for a DK weight thickness. All yarns don't have to be the exact same weight or fiber blend. Be adventurous and freely mix different colors and fibers together! I always use the needle I like with the thickest yarn and use that same needle with thinner yarns for a more airy fabric.

Instructions are written using colors A, B, C, etc… to mark when different colors are used, but feel free to ignore the exact color changes and throw in bits of color and texture whenever you want.

Yardage: Approximately 1000yds / 914m for the two thinner gauge sizes, 1200yds / 1097m for the middle gauge sizes, and 1400yds / 1280m for the thicker gauge sizes .

This sweater is meant to use odd balls and scrap yarn for a patchwork/color blocked effect. If you run out of yarn in one section grab another ball of yarn and keep knitting!

Shown in: Blue/Green Version - A collection of Hedgehog Fibres Merino DK, handspun angora, kidsilk mohair lace, Orkney Angora, and cormo wool

Black/Neutral/Blue Pop Version - Woolfolk Luft (6 skeins for neck, body, and sleeves), Brooklyn Tweed SHELTER (2 skeins of black/white marled for bottom short rows), handspun white angora, Hedgehog Fibres Merino Aran, Jill Draper Makes Stuff Middlefield, Álafoss Létt Lopi

Needles: 40" circular in the size needed to obtain desired gauge
40" spare circular needle same size or smaller
Samples used US 8 / 5mm needles

Notions: 1 stitch marker, tapestry needle, waste yarn

Sample Gauge: 18 sts & 24 rnds = 4" / 10cm in stockinette stitch with DK weight yarn & US 8 / 5mm needles

# sts = 1" / 2.5cm	Chest Circumference	Sleeve Circumference	Recommended Yarn Weight
3.5 sts	56" / 142cm	15" / 38cm	Heavy Worsted/Worsted
4 sts	49" / 124cm	13" / 33cm	Worsted
4.5 sts	43" / 109cm	12" / 30cm	DK
5 sts	39" / 99cm	10.5" / 27cm	Sport/ DK
5.5 sts	36" / 91cm	9.5" / 24cm	Sport/Fingering
6 sts	33" / 84cm	8.5" / 22cm	Fingering/Lace

INSTRUCTIONS

Begin with the RIBBED COWL NECK or if you prefer a simple rounded neckline, CO 96 sts and knit a folded stockinette hem or knit a few garter ridges and skip to YOKE instructions.

RIBBED COWL NECK

Using A, CO 96 sts. Place marker and join to knit in the round.

(K2, p2) to end of rnd.

Work 2x2 ribbing in the rnd until neck measures your desired length. The gray sample cowl neck measures approximately 12" / 30cm. Break color A.

YOKE

Using B, (k12, M1L) 8 times. 104 sts.
K 1 rnd. Keep color B attached. It can be striped throughout the yoke for an accent stripe (shown in blue).

Using C, k 1 rnd.
P 1 rnd.

The following short rows are worked by simply turning the work to the other side.

SHORT ROW SECTION 1

Row 1 (RS): Using C, k to 4 sts before marker, turn to work WS.
Row 2 (WS): K to 4 sts before marker, turn to work RS.

Row 3 (RS): K to 4 sts before last turn, turn to work WS.
Row 4 (WS): K to 4 sts before last turn, turn to work RS.

Repeat last 2 rows 10 more times. Break color C. Slip sts from the left needle onto right needle until you reach the beginning of rnd marker.

Next Rnd: Using B, (k4, yo) 12 times, k8, (yo, k4) 12 times. 128 sts.

K 1 rnd.

SHORT ROW SECTION 2

Row 1 (RS): Using D, k to 5 sts before marker, turn to work WS.
Row 2 (WS): K to 5 sts before marker, turn to work RS.

Row 3 (RS): K to 5 sts before last turn, turn to work WS.
Row 4 (WS): K to 5 sts before last turn, turn to work RS.

Repeat last 2 rows 10 more times. Break color D. Slip sts from the left needle onto right needle until you reach the beginning of rnd marker.

Next Rnd: Using B, (k5, yo) 12 times, k8, (yo, k5) 12 times. 152 sts.

K 1 rnd.

SHORT ROW SECTION 3

Row 1 (RS): Using E, k to 6 sts before marker, turn to work WS.
Row 2 (WS): K to 6 sts before marker, turn to work RS.

Row 3 (RS): K to 6 sts before last turn, turn to work WS.
Row 4 (WS): K to 6 sts before last turn, turn to work RS.

Repeat last 2 rows 10 more times. Break color E. Slip sts from the left needle onto right needle until you reach the beginning of rnd marker.

Next Rnd: Using B, (k6, yo) 12 times, k8, (yo, k6) 12 times. 176 sts.

K 1 rnd.

SHORT ROW SECTION 4

Row 1 (RS): Using F, k to 7 sts before marker, turn to work WS.
Row 2 (WS): K to 7 sts before marker, turn to work RS.

Row 3 (RS): K to 7 sts before last turn, turn to work WS.
Row 4 (WS): K to 7 sts before last turn, turn to work RS.

Repeat last 2 rows 10 more times. Break color F. Slip sts from the left needle onto right needle until you reach the beginning of rnd marker.

Next Rnd: Using B, (k7, yo) 12 times, k8, (yo, k7) 12 times. 200 sts.

K 1 rnd.

SHORT ROW SECTION 5
Row 1 (RS): Using G, k to 8 sts before marker, turn to work WS.
Row 2 (WS): K to 8 sts before marker, turn to work RS.

Row 3 (RS): K to 8 sts before last turn, turn to work WS.
Row 4 (WS): K to 8 sts before last turn, turn to work RS.

Repeat last 2 rows 10 more times. Break color G. Slip sts from the left needle onto right needle until you reach the beginning of rnd marker.

Next Rnd: Using B, (k8, yo) 12 times, k8, (yo, k8) 12 times. 224 sts.

K 1 rnd. Break color B.

BODY
Using H, k92, slip next 40 sts onto waste yarn, CO 12 sts for the underarm using the cable CO method, k92. 196 sts remain.

K 1 rnd.

Using I, k 2 rnds.

Continue knitting stripes in the round (2 rounds of H, 2 rounds of I) until work measures approximately 11" / 28cm from underarm or until the fabric reaches your hip. Include some accent stripes or throw in some seed stitch if you feel like adding color or texture pops to the body of your sweater.

Break colors H & I. Slip the first 20 and last 20 sts of the round (20 sts on both sides of the stitch marker) onto waste yarn. 156 sts remain. Slip 78 sts onto the needle and place marker to mark a new beginning of round location at the other side of the body.

Using J, k78, CO 12 sts for the underarm using the cable CO method, k78. 168 sts.

P 1 rnd.

SHORT ROWS
Row 1 (RS): K to 2 sts before m, turn to work WS.
Row 2 (WS): K to 2 sts before m, turn to work RS.

Row 3 (RS): K to 2 sts before last turn, turn to work WS.
Row 4 (WS): K to 2 sts before last turn, turn to work RS.

Repeat last 2 rows 35 more times.

Next Row (RS): K to m while closing the short row gaps.
Next Rnd: P to end of rnd closing while closing the short row gaps.

K 1 rnd.
P 1 rnd. Break color J.

Continue with the Garter Stitch Border to add a few garter ridges to the bottom of the sweater or skip to the Brioche Border to add some ribbed two-color brioche to your sweater.

GARTER STITCH BORDER
Using K, k 1 rnd.
P 1 rnd.

Repeat last 2 rnds twice more or until the sweater is as long as you like. BO all sts on the next rnd loosely as follows, *k2tog tbl, slip stitch back to left needle, repeat from * until all sts are bound off. Break yarn and pull it through the last stitch. Continue with Sleeves.

BRIOCHE BORDER
Use two new colors for the two-color brioche border. Color A is the foreground color. Color B is the background color.

Rnd 1A: Using A, k to end of rnd.
Rnd 1B: Using B, (sl1yo, p1) to end of rnd.

Rnd 2A: Using A, (brk1, sl1yo) to end of rnd.
Rnd 2B: Using B, (sl1yo, brp1) to end of rnd.

Repeat Rnds 2A & 2B 18 more times or until the border reaches your desired length.

Next Rnd: Using a contrast color, (brk1, k1) to end of rnd.

Create an accent stripe with eyelets or skip ahead to the Folded Hem. You could also bind off with an I-cord bind off if you're ready to knit the sleeves.

Eyelet Rnd (optional): (K2tog, yo) to end of rnd for an eyelet row. Break yarn.

Using a new color, k 15 rnds.

Create a hem by folding the 15 rnds in half. K1 live stitch together with a picked up stitch from 15 rnds below, *k next live stitch together with a picked up stitch from 15 rnds below, pass first stitch on right needle over the most recent stitch to bind off 1, repeat from * until all sts are bound off.

Using any color for the sleeve, slip 40 sts from waste yarn onto needle. K40, CO 12 sts using the cable CO method, place marker. 52 sts.

Knit in the rnd until sleeve measures approximately 19" / 48cm from underarm or until it reaches your desired length. Maintain the 52 sts for simple oversized sleeves or decrease gradually for a more fitted sleeve. The sample with super long striped sleeves measures 38" / 97cm so you can gather and bunch up the sleeves. The striped sleeves are finished with folded stockinette stitch hems.

The sample with dark gray sleeves is finished with a regular bind off for a rolled edge. To bind off, *k2tog tbl, slip stitch onto left needle, repeat from * to end of rnd. Break yarn and pull it through the last stitch.

Weave in ends and block the sweater to smooth the fabric.

ENCHANTED MESA PONCHO

Use the original Enchanted Mesa instructions and modify them into a stylish poncho!

Finished Measurements: 32" / 81cm from neckline to bottom edge, 50" / 127cm body circumference

Yarn: Chunky weight
Hold multiple strands together to get a marled effect.
1 worsted weight wool + 1 fingering weight wool + 1 lace weight mohair held together = chunky weight
Fade your colors together by dropping 1 strand of yarn and replace it with a new strand.

Shown in: Hedgehog Fibres Merino Aran held together with various fingering weight wools and a strand of lace weight mohair/silk. The sample used about 7 skeins of Aran weight yarn (100g each) as the base strand.

Needles: 40" US 11 / 8mm circular

Gauge: 13 sts & 26 rows = 4" 10cm in garter stitch

Modifications: Start by knitting a 3-stitch I-cord 96 rows long with a color pop for the neckline.
Using a new color, pick up and k96 sts along the I-cord edge.
Continue with YOKE instructions.
Work seed stitch instead of stockinette stitch in the round for BODY.
Omit the sleeves and immediately work an I-cord BO after picking up your sleeve sts.

ENCHANTED MESA DRESS

Finished Measurements: 33" / 84cm chest circumference. Length is customizable. Instructions include modification notes on this small dress variation of the original pattern.

Yarn: Fingering weight

Shown in: Hedgehog Fibres Sock Yarn in neutral speckled shades along with a few other fingering weight wools

Yardage: Start with at least 6 colors fading from light to dark along with some color pops. The sample used approximately 350g of the main speckled colors and about 60-70g total for solid color pops, accent stripes, and the background of the brioche border.

Needles: 40" US 4 / 3.5mm

Gauge: 24 sts & 32 rows = 4" / 10cm in stockinette stitch

INSTRUCTIONS

Use the original Enchanted Mesa instructions along with these modifications to knit a small sized dress. These notes are meant to be a guideline to help you customize your Enchanted Mesa garment. Try on the sweater as you knit to get the desired proportions for your body type.

YOKE

Create a 3-stitch I-cord for 96 rows with a contrast color. Pick up and k96 sts along I-cord edge and continue with YOKE instructions.

Use different color pops for the 2-row stripes between the short row wedges. Introduce new main colors as you like throughout the YOKE. Sample shows the first main color in Wedges 1 & 2. There is a second darker main color for Wedges 3 & 4. Only work 4 short row wedges. 200 sts.

Increase 24 sts evenly throughout the next rnd (shown in gold) resulting in 224 sts. K 1 more contrast color rnd.

BODY

Continue with original BODY instructions to separate the first sleeve resulting in 196 sts. Knit in the rnd and start fading into a new color by working 2-row stripes with each color until you are ready to break the old color and use the new color on its own. Continue knitting the BODY in the rnd until it matches the length of the short row YOKE wedges (measured along the long part of the short rows). The sample was knit in the rnd for 50 rnds.

K 2 rnds for a contrast pop (shown in blue).

Separate the second sleeve as instructed in the original pattern.

Continue fading colors as you like and k168 sts in the rnd for about 26cm measured from the underarm or knit in the rnd until fabric reaches your waist. This entire section is like an additional BODY section before knitting the bottom garter stitch short rows.

K 2 rnds with a contrast color.
K 1 rnd with your main color.
P 1 rnd with your main color.

SHORT ROWS

Start the Short Rows section as written. After repeating the short row turns 35 more times, close the short row gaps using a color pop stripe for 2 rnds (shown in pink).

DRESS

You can incorporate the recommended increases and knit the dress as long as you want until working the brioche border.

Using a main color, increase 21 sts evenly throughout the next rnd. 189 total sts.

K 10 rnds.

Next Rnd: (K7, m1) to end of rnd. 216 sts.

K 15 rnds.

Using a contrast color, (k6, yo) to end of row. 252 sts.
K 1 more rnd with contrast color (shown in gold).

K 20 rnds. Continue to fade colors as you like.

Next Rnd: (K7, m1) to end of rnd. 288 sts.

K about 15 rnds.

Using a contrast color, (K8, yo) to end of rnd. 324 sts.
K 1 more rnd using the contrast color (shown in green).

K about 4" / 10cm in the rnd or until you are ready to knit the brioche border.

BRIOCHE BORDER

Follow the BRIOCHE BORDER instructions in the original pattern until the ribbing is as long as you want. Throw in some lace weight mohair for extra fluffy texture. Sample foreground shown in gray with the background in Hedgehog Fibres Pollen (gold).

Finish the bottom edge with an I-cord BO.

SLEEVES

Follow the original sleeve instructions. Gradually decrease sts to create a more fitted/ tapered sleeve. Knit in the rnd until sleeve reaches your desired length. Use an I-cord BO or try some 2x2 ribbing on a smaller needle to finish the sleeve cuff.

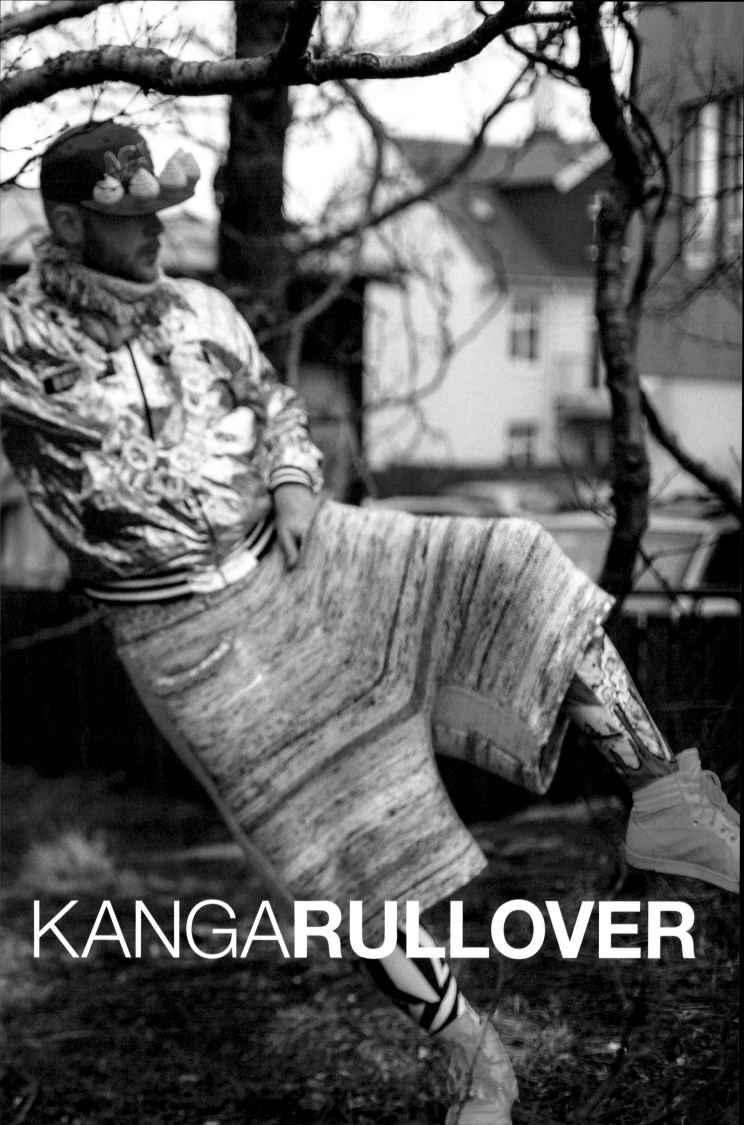

KANGA**RULLOVER**

KANGARULLOVER

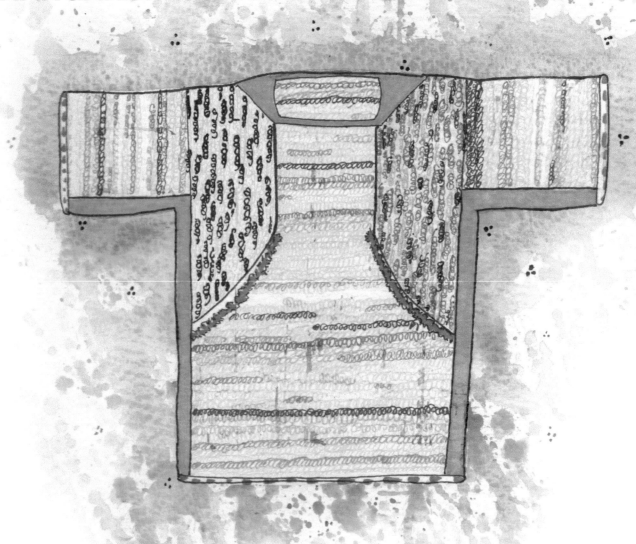

What would a kangaroo look like if it wore the speckled pullover of its dreams? Experience the cozy sensation of the Kangarullover enveloping your body in warmth. This squishy speckled garment is knit with several simple shapes that are seamlessly joined together using Westknits modular knitting techniques.

Hold 2 strands of DK weight yarn together as you fade and stripe your colors.

The front panel features a giant pocket for you to stash all your favorite yarns and treasures. This garment is a great stash buster! Don't be afraid to throw in some fluff and stuff or even some sparkly metallic yarns and bounce like a kangaroo!

Sizes: Small [Large]

Finished Measurements: 44 [48]" / 112 [122] cm chest circumference, 27 [32]" / 69 [81]cm from shoulder to bottom edge, 19 [21]" / 48 [53]cm neck circumference, 18" / 46cm sleeve circumference, sleeve length is customizable. Garment is designed to fit with at least 2-10"/ 5-25cm of positive ease.

Yarn: Chunky weight or DK weight held double

Yardage: Approximately 1000g total of DK weight for Front, Back, Sleeves, and Pocket Lining.
Approximately 200g of DK weight for Left and Right Front panels (shown in blue/yellow & green/pink for Small size)

Approximately 100g of chunky weight or 200g of DK weight (held double) for neck edge, side panels, and I-cord edges (shown in orange for the sides and pink/yellow for I-cord edges on Small Size)

The Small size requires a bit less yardage, but I recommend using a colorful pile of yarns mixed together for generous color possibilities.

Shown in: A variety of DK weight yarns held together including Ístex Álafoss Lopi, Hedgehog Fibres Merino DK, Brooklyn Tweed SHELTER, Walk Collection Merino DK, Republic of Wool DK Merino, Madelinetosh Tosh DK, some fluffy alpaca, sparkly metallic, and fun fur.

Needles: 40" US 10 / 6mm circular

Notions: Tapestry needle

Gauge: 16 sts & 26 rows = 4" / 10cm in garter stitch

INSTRUCTIONS

The black & white sample photos represent the Large sample size. The colorful speckled sample represents the Small sample size.

FRONT

Using 2 strands held together, CO 26 sts.
Next Row (WS): K25, sl1 wyif.

Row 1 (RS): K25, sl1 wyif.
Row 2 (WS): K25, sl1 wyif.

Repeat last 2 rows 28 [34] more times. 30 [36] total garter ridges.

Next Row (RS): Kfb, k to last st, sl1 wyif.
Next Row (WS): Kfb, k to last st, sl1 wyif.

Repeat last 2 rows 23 [29] more times. 54 [66] total garter ridges. 74 [86] sts.

Repeat Rows 1 & 2 30 [36] more times. 84 [102] total garter ridges.

Place 74 [86] sts onto waste yarn.

RIGHT FRONT

Using 2 strands held together and with RS facing, pick up and k30 [36] selvedge sts from the right edge of FRONT piece (along the first 30 [36] garter ridges from FRONT). CO 24 [30] sts using the cable CO method. 54 [66] total sts.
Next Row (WS): K53 [65], sl1 wyif.

Row 1 (RS): Kfb, k to last st, sl1 wyif.
Row 2 (WS): K to last st, sl1 wyif.

Repeat last 2 rows 22 [28] more times. 77 [95] sts. Break yarn and place sts onto waste yarn.

LEFT FRONT

Using 2 strands held together, CO 24 [30] sts. With RS facing, pick up and k30 [36] selvedge sts from the left edge of FRONT piece (along the first 30 [36] garter ridges from FRONT).
Next Row (WS): K53 [65], sl1 wyif.

Row 1 (RS): K to last st, sl1 wyif.
Row 2 (WS): Kfb, k to last st, sl1 wyif.

Repeat last 2 rows 22 [28] more times. 77 [95] sts. Break yarn and place sts onto waste yarn.

Row 1 (RS): Sl1, place yarn in back, kfb, k to last st, sl2 wyif (the last stitch and next selvedge stitch from RIGHT FRONT).
Row 2 (WS): K2tog, kfb, k to last st, ssk (last stitch together with next selvedge stitch from LEFT FRONT).

Repeat Rows 1 & 2 13 [19] more times. 74 [86] sts.

Row 41 (RS): K73 [85], sl1 wyif.
Row 42 (WS): K73 [85], sl1 wyif.

Repeat last 2 rows 80 [90] more times. Break yarn and place sts onto waste yarn. There should be 95 [111] total garter ridges on the RS of BACK piece.

BACK

Using 2 strands of yarn held together, CO 46 sts.
Next Row (WS): K46.

Use this video tutorial to assist with the BACK construction.
https://youtu.be/aXQxHky6V1g

The next rows are worked back and forth while being attached to the RIGHT and LEFT FRONTS. Place a stitch marker in the tenth selvedge stitch from the RIGHT FRONT and the LEFT FRONT (along the diagonal increase edge). These first 10 selvedge stitches will be saved for the neckline. The BACK attachment in Rows 1 & 2 begins with the eleventh selvedge stitch from each FRONT piece.

RIGHT SLEEVE

Row 1 (RS): Using 2 strands of yarn held together and with RS facing, pick up and k16 [10] selvedge sts from BACK. Place next 44 [50] RIGHT FRONT sts from waste yarn onto left needle from left to right so the needle tips meet each other. K50. Turn to work WS. Leave the remaining 33 [45] RIGHT FRONT sts onto waste yarn.

Row 2 (WS): K59, sl1 wyif.

Row 3 (RS): K59, sl1 wyif.
Row 4 (WS): K59, sl1 wyif.

Repeat last 2 rows 30 more times. There should be 32 garter ridges. Break yarn and place sts onto waste yarn.

LEFT SLEEVE

Row 1 (WS): Using 2 strands of yarn held together and with RS facing, k the last 44 [50] sts from LEFT FRONT waste yarn. Leave the first 33 [45] LEFT FRONT sts onto waste yarn. Pick up and k16 [10] selvedge sts from BACK. Turn to work WS.
Row 2 (WS): K59, sl1 wyif.

Row 3 (RS): K59, sl1 wyif.
Row 4 (WS): K59, sl1 wyif.

Repeat last 2 rows 30 more times. There should be 32 garter ridges. Break yarn and place sts onto waste yarn.

POCKET LINING

The beginning of the pocket lining is attached to the cable cast on edges of the LEFT and RIGHT FRONTS.
Using 2 strands of yarn held together, CO 26 sts.
Row 1 (RS): K25, sl1 wyif.

Row 2 (WS): K25, sl1 wyif, pick up 1 stitch from RIGHT FRONT cable CO edge.
Row 3 (RS): K2tog, k to last st, ssk: slip last stitch knit-wise, pick up a stitch from LEFT FRONT cable CO edge and knit those 2 stitches together through the back loop.

Row 4 (WS): Yarn is hanging in front. Sl1, place yarn in back, k24, sl1 wyif, pick up the next stitch from RIGHT FRONT cable CO edge.
Row 5 (RS): K2tog, k24, ssk: slip last stitch knit-wise, pick up the next stitch from LEFT FRONT cable CO edge and knit those 2 stitches together through the back loop.

Repeat last 2 rows 20 [26] more times until all cable CO sts from RIGHT and LEFT FRONTS are attached. Break yarn.

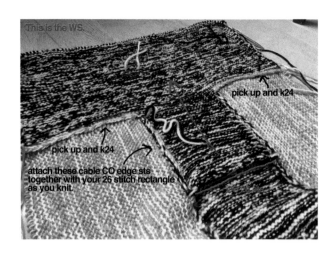

If these instructions were confusing, you can also just CO 26 sts and knit 22 [28] garter ridges and seam the sides of this new rectangle to the cable cast on edges of the RIGHT and LEFT FRONTS.

Next Row (WS): Using 2 strands of yarn held together and with RS facing, pick up and k24 [30] from from LEFT FRONT selvedge, k26 sts, pick up and k24 [30] from RIGHT FRONT selvedge. 74 [86] sts.
Next Row (RS): K85, sl1 wyif.

Next Row (WS): K85, sl1 wyif.
Next Row (RS): K85, sl1 wyif.

Repeat last 2 rows 30 [34] more times. The POCKET LINING and front piece should now be the same length.

Next Row (WS): Place 74 [86] sts from FRONT piece onto a spare circular needle. Attach 74 [86] sts from FRONT piece together with the [74] 86 POCKET LINING sts by knitting 1 FRONT stitch together with 1 POCKET LINING stitch. Knit the 2 pieces together as pictured to end of row. If this attachment is confusing, you can also bind off all pocket lining sts and bind off all front sts and sew those 2 edges together to close the bottom of the sweater.

Break yarn and place 74 [86] sts onto waste yarn.

RIGHT STRIP
These next sections are the right and left long solid strips on the sides and underarm. They are knit as a long rectangle while being attached to the selvedge and live sts.

Using 2 strands of yarn held together, CO 12 sts. Sample shows the same color held together for a bold solid strip.
Next Row (WS): K11, sl1 wyif.

Row 1 (RS): K11, sl1 wyif, pick up the first selvedge stitch by the sts on waste yarn from RIGHT SLEEVE.
Row 2 (WS): K2tog, k10, ssk: slip last stitch knit-wise, pick up a stitch from RIGHT SLEEVE selvedge and knit those 2 stitches together through the back loop.

Row 3 (RS): Sl1 wyif, place yarn in back, k10, sl1 wyif, pick up the next stitch from RIGHT SLEEVE selvedge.

Row 4 (WS): K2tog, k10, ssk: slip last stitch purl-wise, pick up a stitch from RIGHT SLEEVE selvedge and knit those 2 stitches together through the back loop.

Repeat last 2 rows until all selvedge sts from RIGHT SLEEVE are attached, then continue knitting and attaching the strip down the side of the garment.
Instead of picking up a selvedge stitch at the end of Row 3, you will slip a live RIGHT FRONT stitch from waste yarn. The ssk at the end of Row 4 will be attached to the BACK selvedge sts.
Once all RIGHT FRONT sts are attached, continue Rows 3 & 4 while attaching them to the FRONT and BACK selvedge sts.

When you reach the FRONT & POCKET LINING layers, pick up an extra stitch at the end of Row 3 so you pick up a FRONT selvedge stitch and a POCKET LINING stitch. Then, you will k3tog at the beginning of Row 4.

RS: slip last stitch and a picked up stitch from FRONT & POCKET LINING

WS: slip last stitch and a picked up POCKET LINING & FRONT selvedge stitch and knit them all together tbl

Once you reach the bottom edge, place 12 sts onto waste yarn.

LEFT STRIP

This is the same strip and attachment method as the RIGHT STRIP.

Using 2 strands of yarn held together, CO 12 sts.
Next Row (WS): K11, sl1 wyif.

Row 1 (RS): K11, sl1 wyif, pick up the first selvedge stitch by the sts on waste yarn from LEFT SLEEVE.
Row 2 (WS): K2tog, k10, ssk: slip last stitch knit-wise, pick up a stitch from LEFT SLEEVE selvedge and knit those 2 sts together through the back loop.

Row 3 (RS): Sl1 wyif, place yarn in back, k10, sl1 wyif, pick up the next stitch from LEFT SLEEVE selvedge.
Row 4 (WS): K2tog, k10, ssk: slip last stitch knit-wise, pick up a stitch from LEFT SLEEVE selvedge and knit those 2 sts together through the back loop.

Repeat last 2 rows until all selvedge sts from LEFT SLEEVE are attached, then continue knitting and attaching the strip down the side of the garment.
Instead of picking up a selvedge stitch at the end of Row 4, you will slip a live stitch knit-wise from the LEFT FRONT waste yarn. The k2tog at the beginning of Row 4 will be attached to the BACK selvedge sts.
Once all LEFT FRONT sts are attached, continue Rows 3 & 4 while attaching them to the FRONT and BACK selvedge sts.
When you reach the FRONT & POCKET LINING layers, turn the ssk into a sssk by picking up a selvedge stitch from FRONT and a selvedge stitch from POCKET LINING.

Once you reach the bottom edge, break yarn. Use 2 new strands of yarn held together to knit the next RS row followed by an I-cord BO.

Next Row (RS): K12, k74 [86] BACK sts from waste yarn, k12. Turn to BO on the WS.
Next Row (WS): CO 3 sts using the cable CO method, *k2, k2tog tbl, repeat from * until all SIDE STRIP and BACK sts are bound off. Place 74 [86] FRONT sts onto circular needle and continue binding them off the same way. Break yarn and pull it through the last 3 sts.

POCKET TRIM

Choose a color to decorate the diagonal edge of the pocket opening. Small size shown in neon fun fur and yellow I-cord.

(Pick up and k4, m1) along diagonal increase edge of FRONT pocket.
Next Row (WS): K all sts.

BO all sts on the RS using an I-cord BO.

Repeat POCKET TRIM instructions for the other diagonal pocket opening.

SLEEVE TRIM

Place all sleeve sts and 12 Side Strip sts onto needle. Using 2 colors held together and with RS facing, BO all sts using an I-cord BO.

LEFT NECK TRIANGLE

Using 2 strands of yarn held together (Small sample used orange yarn doubled) and with RS facing, pick up and k2 sts into the corner where the BACK intersects with the LEFT FRONT. Turn to work WS.

Next Row (WS): K1, ssk (next st together with a picked up st from the BACK CO edge).
Next Row (RS): Sl1 wyif then place the yarn in back to knit, M1L, sl1 wyif, pick up a selvedge stitch from LEFT FRONT and slip it onto the right needle.
Next Row (WS): K2tog (the picked up selvedge stitch together with the slipped neck stitch), kfb, ssk (next st together with a picked up st from the BACK CO edge). 4 sts.

Row 1 (RS): Sl1 wyif then place the yarn in back to knit, k to last st, sl1 wyif, pick up next selvedge stitch from LEFT FRONT and slip it onto the right needle.
Row 2 (WS): K2tog (the picked up selvedge stitch together with the slipped neck stitch), M1L, k to last st, ssk (next st together with the next picked up st from the BACK CO edge). 5 sts.

Repeat last 2 rows 8 more times. 13 sts. Break yarn and place 13 sts onto waste yarn.

RIGHT NECK TRIANGLE

Using 2 strands of yarn held together and with RS facing, pick up and k2 sts into the corner where the BACK intersects with the RIGHT FRONT. Turn to work WS.

Next Row (WS): K1, ssk (next st together with a picked up selvedge st from RIGHT FRONT).
Next Row (RS): Sl1 wyif then place the yarn in back to knit, M1L, sl1 wyif, pick up a stitch from the BACK CO edge and slip it onto the right needle.
Next Row (WS): K2tog (the picked up BACK stitch together with the slipped neck stitch), kfb, ssk (next st together with a picked up selvedge st from RIGHT FRONT). 4 sts.

Row 1 (RS): Sl1 wyif then place the yarn in back to knit, kfb, k to last st, sl1 wyif, pick up a stitch from the BACK CO edge and slip it onto the right needle.
Row 2 (WS): K2tog (the picked up BACK stitch together with the slipped neck stitch), k to last st, ssk (next st together with a picked up selvedge st from RIGHT FRONT). 5 sts.

Repeat last 2 rows 8 more times. 13 sts.

Next Row (RS): K13, pick up and k remaining BACK sts, k13 sts from LEFT NECK TRIANGLE, pick up and k24 from FRONT neck edge. BO all sts using an I-cord BO.

FINISHING

Break yarn, weave in ends, and fill the pockets with your favorite treasures!

Large Size
Yarn: Woolfolk Får held double (black & white)
Worsted weight wool (gold) held together with
fingering weight wool (yellow)

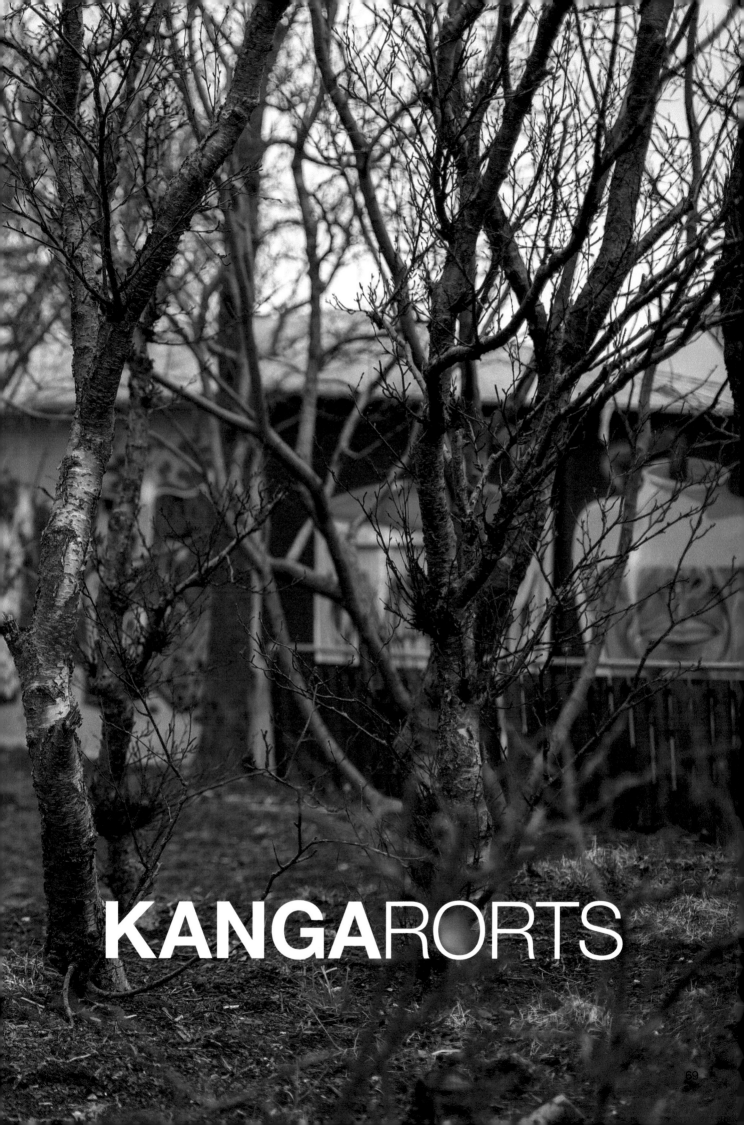

KANGARORTS

KANGARORTS

Knit some cozy shorts using two strands of yarn held together. The front and back pieces are knit flat with simple shaping so the inseam and crotch depth are easy to customize. Hold DK weight yarns double to eat up your leftover stash for a chunky marled fabric. The waist incorporates a folded hem with an elastic band. Color pop side panels and afterthought pockets add a final splash to these comfy shorts.

Sizes: S [M, L, XL] Sample shown in size L on a 34" / 86cm waist.

Finished Measurements: 23 [28, 32, 38]" / 58 [71, 81, 97]cm waist with elastic band relaxed, elastic band stretches to fit up to 31 [36, 40, 46]" / 79 [91, 102, 117]cm waist. Length is customizable.

Yarn: Chunky weight or DK weight held double.

Yardage: Approximately 900 [1000, 1100, 1200]g total or 1980 [2200, 2420, 2640]yds / 1811 [2012, 2213, 2414]m total with yarn held doubled. You will require half the yardage if you are holding a single strand of chunky weight.

Side & inseam panels require 1 skein of DK weight (100g) held double.

Shown in: A variety of speckled & solid DK weight yarns held together. Add fun fur if you're feeling funky!

Needles: 40" US 10 / 6mm needle

Notions: 4 stitch markers, tapestry needle, 2.5" / 6cm wide elastic band long enough to fit around your waist

Gauge: 16 sts & 26 rows = 4" / 10cm in garter stitch

INSTRUCTIONS

The construction begins by creating the identical garter stitch front and back pieces first. Then the waistband is picked up and knit in the round for a folded hem. Finally, the color pop side panels and inseam panels are knit while being attached to the front and back sections. An I-cord bind off finishes the bottom of each leg. The afterthought pockets are added after all the other sections are finished.

FRONT
Using 2 strands of DK weight held together, CO 52 [62, 72, 82] sts.

Next Row (WS): K34, pm, k4, pm, k33, sl1 wyif.

Row 1 (RS): K to last st, sl1 wyif.
Row 2 (WS): K to last st, sl1 wyif.
Row 3 (RS): K to m, M1R, slm, k4, slm, M1L, k to last st, sl1 wyif.
Row 4 (WS): K to last st, sl1 wyif.

Repeat last 4 rows until crotch depth reaches your desired length. The Large sample size repeated Rows 1-4 22 times resulting in 118 total stitches for a baggy oversized look with crotch depth of 15.5" / 39cm. I recommend a crotch depth of 10-12" / 25-30cm for the Small or Medium size.

Colors: Play with fading and striping your colors together as you knit the garter stitch fabric. Try changing 1 strand of yarn at a time to fade and blend your colors together.
The sample changed one of the colors every 2-10 rows.

LEGS
Divide the row in half. Knit half the stitches and place the other half onto waste yarn. For example, the sample has 118 sts so k59, and place the other 59 onto waste yarn.

Knit the first half of the stitches back and forth in garter stitch while slipping the last stitch of every row with yarn in front. Knit the leg until it reaches your desired length. Sample leg/inseam measures 10" / 25cm. Place all sts onto waste yarn.

Place the other half of the stitches onto your needle to knit the other leg as long as the first leg. Don't forget to slip the last stitch of every row with yarn in front. Place all sts onto waste yarn.

BACK
Repeat all Front & Leg instructions for an identical Back piece.

WAISTBAND
With RS facing and 2 strands of yarn held together, (pick up and k5, skip 1 stitch) from Front CO edge so you get 5 picked up and knit sts for every 6 sts resulting in a more fitted waistband, CO 12 stitches using the cable cast on method, (pick up and k5, skip 1 stitch) from Back CO edge, CO 12 sts using the cable cast on method. 112 [128, 144, 162] total sts. Place marker and join to knit in the rnd.

K26 rnds or until waistband measures 5" / 13cm.

Sew a 2.5" / 6cm wide piece of elastic into a circle for the waistband. The length of the elastic should be fitted when it's around your waist.
Recommended Elastic band length: 23 [28, 32, 38]" / 58 [71, 81, 97]cm
Fold the stockinette fabric in half to begin creating the folded hem while trapping the elastic waistband inside.

K2tog (1 live stitch together with a picked up stitch from the WS of the Front edge), *k2tog (next live stitch together withe a picked up stitch from the WS of the Front edge), pass first stitch over to BO 1 stitch, repeat from * until all stitches are bound off to create the folded hem.

If you are having trouble trapping the elastic waistband inside the hem, you can create the folded hem first. Before you finish binding off the last few sts, shove the elastic into the folded hem and sew it closed.

SIDE PANELS

Follow this video tutorial to assist with the side panels...
https://youtu.be/yLSYAxNgNt8

Using 2 strands of yarn held together and with RS facing, pick up and k12 sts from cable CO edge of the waistband. This pick up should be in the gap between the front and back pieces.

Next Row (WS): K12.

Row 1 (RS): Sl1 wyif, place yarn in back, k10, sl2 wyif (the last stitch and a picked up selvedge stitch), turn to work WS.

Row 2 (WS): K2tog, k10, ssk (slip the last stitch knit-wise, slip the selvedge stitch by diving into the wrong side of the selvedge stitch, knit those 2 sts together tbl), turn to work RS.

Repeat last 2 rows to attach the side panel to the front and back pieces until you reach the bottom of the leg. Place 12 sts onto waste yarn.

Repeat all Side Panel instructions for the other side.

INSEAM

Using 2 strands of yarn held together, CO 12 sts.

Next Row (WS): K12.

Row 1 (RS): Sl1 wyif, place yarn in back, k10, sl2 wyif (the last stitch and a picked up selvedge stitch from the bottom of one of the legs), turn to work WS.

Row 2 (WS): K2tog, k10, ssk (slip the last stitch knit-wise, slip a leg selvedge stitch by diving into the wrong side of the selvedge stitch, knit those 2 sts together tbl), turn to work RS.

Repeat last 2 rows to create a rectangular panel on the inseam of one leg and then continue repeating Rows 1 & 2 to form the inseam of the other leg. You should end at the bottom edge of the other leg. Place 12 sts onto waste yarn.

FINISHING

Place all leg, side panel, and inseam sts from one leg onto a circular needle. Using 2 strands of yarn and with RS facing, k all sts. BO all sts with an I-cord bind off.

I-cord BO: Cast on 3 sts using the cable cast on method, *k2, k2tog tbl, slip 3 sts onto left needle, repeat from * until all sts are bound off. Break yarn and pull it through the remaining 3 sts.

Repeat I-cord BO instructions for the other leg. One leg will have 12 live sts from the inseam and the other leg will have the cast on edge from the Inseam. You need to pick up and k12 Inseam sts from the leg that has the cast on edge from the Inseam instructions.

Afterthought Pockets

Cut 1 stitch from the Front piece approximately 2.5" / 6cm below the beginning of the waistband.

Unravel the row while placing the live sts from the top and bottom onto a circular needle. Continue unraveling and rescuing the sts until the opening is approximately 6" / 15cm wide.

Large Size
Yarn: Madelinetosh Tosh DK and other wool/alpaca DK yarns held double, mohair boucle, sparkly novelty yarns, fun fur & mohair/silk

BO the live sts from the bottom of the pocket opening with an I-cord BO. The sample pocket shows 2 rows of fun fur knit back and forth before the I-cord BO for an extra color pop.

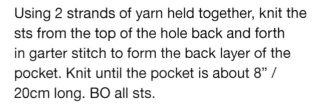

Using 2 strands of yarn held together, knit the sts from the top of the hole back and forth in garter stitch to form the back layer of the pocket. Knit until the pocket is about 8" / 20cm long. BO all sts.

Seam the sides and bottom of this new rectangle onto the inside of the front piece to form the pocket.

Repeat all pocket instructions for the second pocket. Weave in the ends.

MARLED **MAGIC** SWEATER

MARLED MAGIC SWEATER

Dive into your yarn collection and experiment with splashy color combinations for this modular marled sweater. This swingy garment uses two strands of yarn held together throughout the entire project. All sections are picked up and attached while you knit so there is minimal seaming. The only two seams are on each side, but you can use a three-needle bind off to avoid sewing! Most sections are knit with seed stitch, garter stitch, mesh, or brioche. The color and texture changes are simple and addicting so you are motivated to finish each section. Mix all your fingering and lace weight yarns together to achieve your own one-of-a-kind artistic color collage!

Sizes: Small [Large]
Sizes are achieved with different gauges. The longer dress (Small green sample & Large neon sample) is achieved by picking up stitches around the bottom edge and knitting mesh so it can be as long as you want.

Finished Measurements: 28 [30]" / 72 [76]cm long from top neck to bottom back, 20 [21]" / 51 [53]cm neck circumference, 54 [72]" / 137 [183]cm wingspan from cuff to cuff, 71 [86]" /

180 [218]cm hip circumference. This garment is designed to fit with super generous positive ease. Cuff length is customizable.

Dress version (sample with dark blue neckline and cuffs) measures 28" / 71cm along center striped panel from neckline to bottom front edge & 44" / 112cm along center back from neckline to bottom back edge.

Yarn: Sport or DK [DK or Worsted] weight.

Small Size
Hold 1 strand of fingering weight together with 1 strand of lace weight or hold 2 strands of lace weight together to achieve the smaller size.

Large Size
Hold 2 strands of fingering weight together or hold 1 strand of fingering weight and 1 strand of lace weight mohair together for the larger size.

Yardage: Sweater Version - approximately 800g total. Dress Version - approximately 950g total.

Shown in: A variety of fingering and lace weight yarns. I used mostly Hedgehog Fibres Sock, Skinny Singles,Sporty Merino, and Kidsilk lace. Sweater with orange cuffs also used paper, cotton, and silk yarns from Habu.

Needles: Two 40" US 6 [8] / 4 [5]mm circular 40" US 5 [7] / 3.75 [4.5]mm circular

Notions: Tapestry needle, spare circular needle for holding stitches.

Gauge: 23 [20] sts & 48 [40] rows = 4" / 10cm in garter stitch

Pattern Notes: Use these marled techniques for blending your colors together.

Standard Marl
Hold 2 strands of yarn together. Maintain these colors for the entire section.

Steady Marl
Hold 2 stands of yarn together. Always keep 1 strand the same color. Only stripe the second strand of yarn.

Fading Marl
Hold 2 strands of yarn together. Only change 1 strand at a time, but you can substitute colors with either strand of yarn at anytime. Blend and fade your colors together.

INSTRUCTIONS

SECTION 1 - Mesh - Bottom of Left Front

Use this video to assist with the written instructions for sections 1 & 2…
https://youtu.be/1mOwiE_GIJc

Color: I recommend doing a **Steady Marl** for SECTION 1. You will always hold 2 strands together. For a Steady Marl, always keep 1 strand of yarn the same color. Only stripe the second strand of yarn, changing colors every 2, 4, or 6 rows.

A **Classic Marl** is also a nice choice for SECTION 1 if you want to keep working with the same 2 colors held together for the entire mesh section. If you do a classic marl then you can ignore the note about striping/breaking your yarn and leaving the long yarn tails.

You can also do a **Fading Marl** if you want to stripe and change both strands of yarn, but I personally like the Steady Marl for SECTION 1 and save the Fading Marl technique for SECTION 2.

All color notes are just suggestions. I encourage you to follow your color instincts and find color combinations that you love.

Yardage: You will need approximately 95yds / 87m of each strand for SECTION 1. Yardage notes are approximate and vary depending on gauge and yarn type.

Using 2 strands held together, CO 40 sts.

P 1 row.

Row 1 (RS): (YO, k2tog) to end of row.
Row 2 (WS): P all sts.

Repeat last 2 rows 49 more times.

As you repeat your rows, stripe your colors by changing 1 strand at a time. Stripe colors every 2, 4 or 6 rows for frequent stripes. Change colors at the beginning of a WS row.

Don't change colors on the RS rows because it will look untidy next to the YO. When you break your yarn and start a new color, leave a tail that hangs 8-10" / 20-25cm past the CO edge. As you introduce more stripes and the length of SECTION 1 gets longer, leave a longer tail of yarn so that all the yarn ends hang to same length past the CO edge. If you are striping colors, it's important to break your yarn and leave a long tail hanging. DO NOT weave in your ends as you go for SECTION 1. You can braid your ends together later.

There should be 50 total rows of yarn over holes. Break yarn and place 40 sts onto a spare circular needle that is the same size or smaller than your working needle. You can also just leave the 40 sts onto your current needle, but be careful not to knit them during the next section. These 40 sts will be used again later in the project.

SECTION 2 - Seed Stitch - Left Front

Color: I recommend doing the **Fading Marl** technique for SECTION 2. I recommend weaving in your ends as you go for this section or knit the ends into the fabric as you introduce new colors.

Yardage: You will need approximately 240yds / 219m of each strand for SECTION 2, but I encourage you to stripe colors and use little bits of several colors for the Fading Marl technique. Yardage notes are approximate and vary depending on gauge and yarn type.

With RS facing, you are going to begin picking up and knitting sts along the left edge of SECTION 1 starting at the upper left corner next to the last row you just worked. (Pick up and and k3, m1) 17 times along the left edge of SECTION 1. You should be picking up 1 stitch next to each yarn over hole. 68 sts.

Next Row (WS): K1, k2tog, (k1, p1) to last st, sl1 wyif. 67 sts.

Row 1 (RS): Kfb, (p1, k1) to last 2 sts, p1, sl1 wyif. 68 sts.
Row 2 (WS): K1, k2tog, (p1, k1) to last st, sl1 wyif. 67 sts.
Row 3 (RS): Kfb, (k1, p1) to last 2 sts, k1, sl1 wyif. 68 sts.
Row 4 (WS): K1, k2tog, (k1, p1) to last st, sl1 wyif. 67 sts.

Repeat last 4 rows 57 more times. There should be 60 selvedge stitches on each edge and 67 total sts.

Here is an example of the Fading Marl technique for SECTION 2. Both strands of yarn are changing, but only change 1 strand at a time. I recommend working with 2 colors held together for a minimum of 3 rows. Change colors frequently for quick color transitions or create a slow gradual fade by working more rows between color changes.

Use this video to assist with the written instructions for sections 3 & 4…
https://youtu.be/IvTaf0xx1uM

SECTION 3 - Brioche or Seed Stitch - Left Back

Color: For SECTION 3, choose between the brioche option OR continue with seed stitch as you decrease and create a triangle. The brioche option is my personal favorite for this section.

I recommend doing a **Steady Marl** or **Standard Marl** for SECTION 3 brioche.

If you decide to work with seed stitch instead of brioche for SECTION 3, continue with the same color idea you were using in SECTION 2. You can also choose 2 different colors for SECTION 3 seed stitch if you want a contrast or color pop.

If you have mohair, the brioche section is a nice place to use that fuzzy texture. I recommend holding 1 strand of mohair together with 1 strand of fingering weight wool throughout the entire section. If you would like to stripe or fade colors, try using the same color of mohair and change your second strand of yarn to get a light to dark fade. If you are not working with mohair, continue using your other fingering weight yarns.

Yardage: You will need approximately 155yds / 142m of each strand for SECTION 3. Yardage notes are approximate and vary depending on gauge and yarn type.

Continue working with the 67 sts from SECTION 2, but you can break your yarn and work with 2 new colors held together for SECTION 3.

BRIOCHE VERSION

Always hold two strands together. Each side is worked once for the one-color brioche technique. You will hold two strands together that act as one yarn. This feels a bit different than many of my other two-color brioche designs because there is no sliding of stitches after you work one side. In this section, turn your work after each row to achieve the reversible squishy ribbing.

Row 1 (RS): K66, sl1 wyif.
Row 2 (WS): (K1, sl1yo) to last st, sl1 wyif.

Row 3 (RS): K1, (brk1, sl1yo) to last 4 sts, brRsldec, sl1 wyif.
Row 4 (WS): K1, sl1yo, (brk1, sl1yo) to last st, sl1 wyif.
Row 5 (RS): K1, (brk1, sl1yo) to last 2 sts, brk1, sl1 wyif.
Row 6 (WS): K1, sl1yo, (brk1, sl1yo) to last st, sl1 wyif.

Repeat last 4 rows 30 more times. 5 sts remain.

Next Row (RS): K1, brRsldec, sl1 wyif. 3 sts.
Next Row (WS): K1, sl1yo, sl1 wyif. Break yarn and pull it through the remaining 3 sts.

Continue to SECTION 4.

SEED STITCH VERSION

Always hold 2 strands of yarn together.

Row 1 (RS): (K1, p1) to last st, sl1 wyif.
Row 2 (WS): K1, k2tog, (p1, k1) to last 2 sts, p1, sl1 wyif.
Row 3 (RS): (K1, p1) to last 2 sts, k1, sl1 wyif.
Row 4 (WS): K1, k2tog, (k1, p1) to last st, sl1 wyif.

Repeat last 4 rows 30 more times. 5 sts remain.

Next Row (RS): (K1, p1) twice, sl1 wyif.
Next Row (WS): K1, k2tog, p1, sl1 wyif. 4 sts.
Next Row (RS): K1, p1, k1, sl1 wyif.
Next Row (WS): K1, k2tog, sl1 wyif. Break yarn and pull it through the remaining 3 sts.

Continue to SECTION 4.

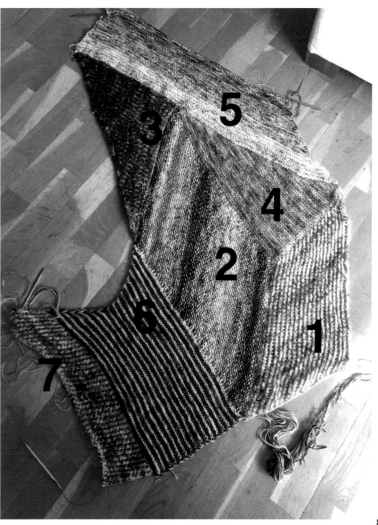

SECTION 4 - Garter Stitch Short Rows - Left Sleeve Triangle

Color: For SECTION 4, I recommend doing a **Steady Marl** or **Standard Marl**. This is another small section so it could be nice to accent this piece with a color pop or create contrast from the other sections. For example, if SECTIONS 1 & 2 are lighter, try making SECTION 4 darker. If you have similar colors in all your sections they may start to blend together which is fine, but if you like a bold contrasting look, then you can color block or accent these new sections with new colors or contrasting shades of color.

SECTION 4 is another nice small section for mohair. If you used mohair for SECTION 3 you could use the same color mohair, but hold it together with different colors for this garter stitch section. You can use a new color of mohair as well if you want more color contrast from SECTION 3.

Yardage: You will need approximately 85yds / 78m of each strand for SECTION 4. Yardage notes are approximate and vary depending on gauge and yarn type.

Place the 40 sts from SECTION 1 onto a circular needle. If your 40 sts are already on a circular needle, you can continue using that needle to pick up and knit sts for SECTION 4.

Using 2 new strands of yarn held together and with RS facing, pick up and knit stitches along the increase edge of SECTION 2 starting at the intersection of SECTION 1 & 2 as follows, *pick up and k3 sts (1 stitch into each selvedge stitch), m1, repeat from * 19 more times. 80 sts. Turn to work WS.

Start picking up stitches here

You will work back and forth in garter stitch while attaching SECTION 4 to the 40 sts from SECTION 1 so make sure your SECTION 1 sts are on a circular needle.

Next Row (WS): k79, ssk (slip the last stitch knit-wise, slip a stitch from SECTION 1 knit-wise, knit those 2 sts together tbl). Turn to work RS.

Row 1 (RS): Sl1 wyif, place yarn in back to knit, k to last 2 sts, turn to work WS.
Row 2 (WS): K to last SECTION 4 st, ssk (slip the last SECTION 4 stitch knit-wise, slip the next stitch from SECTION 1 knit-wise, knit those 2 sts together tbl). Turn to work RS.

Row 3 (RS): Sl1 wyif, place yarn in back to knit, k to 2 sts before last turn, turn to work WS.
Row 4 (WS): K to last SECTION 4 st, ssk (slip the last SECTION 4 stitch knit-wise, slip the next stitch from SECTION 1 knit-wise, knit those 2 sts together tbl). Turn to work RS.

Repeat last 2 rows 37 more times.

Make sure that you don't accidentally knit across all of the SECTION 1 sts on the WS. On the WS, you will always knit until you reach 1 stitch before the next SECTION 1 mesh stitch like the video demonstrates. After repeating Rows 3 & 4 37 more times, all 40 sts from SECTION 1 should be connected to SECTION 4.

Next Row (RS): Sl1 wyif, k all sts while closing the short row gaps. Break yarn and place 80 sts onto waste yarn or a spare circular needle.

The remaining sections use similar small amounts of yardage. Experiment with colors and stripes and have fun!

SECTION 5 - Knit Purl Ridges - Left Back/ Sleeve

Color: I recommend doing a **Fading Marl** for this large section. I changed 1 strand of yarn every 12 rows (3 RS ridges).

Row 1 (RS): Using 2 new strands of yarn and with RS facing, K80 sts from SECTION 4, pick up and k65 sts from SECTION 3 brioche edge (1 stitch for every selvedge stitch). 145 sts.
Row 2 (WS): K to last 3 sts, k2tog, sl1 wyif.

Row 3 (RS): K1, p to last st, sl1 wyif.
Row 4 (WS): K1, p to last 3 sts, p2tog, sl1 wyif.
Row 5 (RS): K to last st, sl1 wyif.
Row 6 (WS): K to last 3 sts, k2tog, sl1 wyif.

Repeat last 4 rows 17 more times, then repeat Row 3 once more. 108 sts. Break yarn and place all sts onto a spare circular needle or waste yarn.

SECTION 6 - Garter Stitch Stripes - Front Center

Color: I recommend doing 2-row stripes for this garter stitch section. SECTION 6 will form the front center of the sweater. I held 2 dark strands together for 2 rows and 2 light strands together for 2 rows.

Row 1 (RS): Using 2 new strands of yarn, (pick up and k3, m1) 20 times along SECTION 2 seed stitch selvedge. 80 sts.
Row 2 (WS): K to last 3 sts, k2tog, sl1 wyif.

Start striping your colors for 2 rows each if you would like vertical stripes on the front center of your sweater.

Row 3 (RS): K to last st, sl1 wyif.
Row 4 (WS): K to last 3 sts, k2tog, sl1 wyif.

Repeat last 2 rows 14 more times. 64 sts.

Row 33 (RS): Kfb, k to last st, sl1 wyif.
Row 34 (WS): K to last st, sl1 wyif.

Repeat last 2 rows 15 more times while continuing to stripe colors. 80 sts. Break yarn.

SECTION 7 - Mesh - Right Front

Color: This is another mesh lace section. You can use a similar color technique like you did for SECTION 1 or choose new colors to create the large mesh panel for the right front.

Continue working with the 80 sts from SECTION 6 using 2 new strands of yarn held together.

Row 1 (RS): K all sts.
Row 2 (WS): P all sts.

Row 3 (RS): (YO, k2tog) to end of row.
Row 4 (WS): P all sts.

Repeat last 2 rows 38 more times. There should be 39 yarn over holes in each column. Break yarn after your last WS row.

As you repeat your rows, stripe your colors like you did for SECTION 1 leaving the long yarn tails at the end of RS rows. If you're striping colors, DO NOT weave in your ends as you go for this section. You can braid your ends later.

SECTION 8 - Knit Purl Short Row Ridges - Right Sleeve Triangle

Color: I recommend doing a **Standard Marl** for this small short row section.

Continue working with the 80 sts from SECTION 7 Mesh. Use 2 new strands of yarn.

Row 1 (RS): K to last st, sl1 wyif.
Row 2 (WS): K to last 2 sts, turn to work RS.

Row 3 (RS): Sl1 purl-wise, p to last st, sl1 wyif.
Row 4 (WS): K1, p to 2 sts before last turn, turn to work RS.
Row 5 (RS): Sl1 knit-wise, k to last st, sl1 wyif.
Row 6 (WS): K to 2 sts before last turn, turn to work RS.

Repeat last 4 rows 17 more times, then repeat Rows 3-5 once more. There should be 19 ridges on the RS. Break yarn and place 80 sts onto a spare circular needle or waste yarn.

SECTION 9 - Seed Stitch - Right Back Triangle

Color: I recommend doing a **Fading Marl** for the seed stitch section.

You will pick up and knit sts from the SECTION 7 Mesh yarn over edge in the following row. There should be 39 yarn over loops.

Row 1 (RS): Using 2 new strands of yarn, (pick up and k1 yarn over loop, m1) 6 times, (pick up and k2 yarn over loops, m1, pick up and k1 yarn over loop, m1) 11 times from the yarn over edge of SECTION 7 Mesh. 67 sts.
Row 2 (WS): (K1, p1) to last 3 sts, k2tog, sl1 wyif. 66 sts.

Row 3 (RS): K1, (k1, p1) to last st, sl1 wyif.
Row 4 (WS): (K1, p1) to last 4 sts, k1, k2tog, sl1 wyif.
Row 5 (RS): (K1, p1) to last st, sl1 wyif.
Row 6 (WS): (K1, p1) to last 3 sts, k2tog, sl1 wyif.

Repeat last 4 rows 30 more times. 4 sts.

Next Row (RS): K1, k1, p1, sl1 wyif.
Next Row (WS): K1, k2tog, sl1 wyif.
Next Row (RS): K1, p1, sl1 wyif.
Next Row (WS): K3tog.

Break yarn and pull it through the last stitch.

SECTION 10 - Brioche - Right Back/Sleeve

Color: I recommend doing a **Steady Marl** for this large brioche section. I used 1 strand of light gray lace weight mohair held together with a darker gray fingering weight wool. I used 3 shades of wool for a subtle fade from light to dark while the mohair color was held throughout the entire section.

Row 1 (RS): Using 2 new strands of yarn, pick up and k65 selvedge sts from the left edge of SECTION 9 Seed Stitch (the straight edge without decreases from SECTION 9), continue to work across the 80 sts from SECTION 8 as follows, (k2tog, yo) 38 times, k3, sl1 wyif. 145 sts.
Row 2 (WS): (K1, sl1yo) to last st, sl1 wyif.

Row 3 (RS): K1, (brk1, sl1yo) to last 4 sts, brRsldec, sl1 wyif.
Row 4 (WS): (K1, sl1yo) to last st, sl1 wyif.
Row 5 (RS): K1, (brk1, sl1yo) to last 2 sts, brk1, sl1 wyif.
Row 6 (WS): (K1, sl1yo) to last st, sl1 wyif.

Repeat last 4 rows 17 more times. 109 sts. Break yarn and place all sts onto a spare circular needle or waste yarn.

SECTION 11 - Seed Stitch - Bottom Right Front

Color: I recommend doing a **Fading Marl** for this seed stitch section.

(pick up and k2, m1) 20 times along SECTION 7 mesh edge for 60 total sts.

Row 1 (RS): Using 2 new strands of yarn, (pick up and k2, m1) 20 times from SECTION 7 Mesh edge. 60 sts.
Row 2 (WS): (K1, p1) to last 2 sts, k1, ssk (last stitch together with a picked up selvedge stitch from SECTION 8).

Row 3 (RS): Sl1 wyif, place yarn in back, M1L, (k1, p1) to last st, sl1 wyif.
Row 4 (WS): K1, k2tog, (p1, k1) to last 2 sts, p1, ssk (last stitch together with the next picked up selvedge stitch from SECTION 8).
Row 5 (RS): Sl1 wyif, place yarn in back, M1L, (p1, k1) to last st, sl1 wyif.
Row 6 (WS): K1, k2tog, (k1, p1) to last 2 sts, k1, ssk (last stitch together with the next picked up selvedge stitch from SECTION 8).

Repeat last 4 rows 35 more times. The new seed stitch should now be attached to all selvedge stitches from SECTION 8. Break yarn.

SECTION 12 - Garter Stitch Short Rows - Right Side

Color: I recommend doing a **Standard Marl** for this seed stitch section.

This Short Row section continues with the 60 sts from the previous Seed Stitch row in SECTION 11. Use 2 new strands of yarn.

Row 1 (RS): K59, sl1 wyif.
Row 2 (WS): kfb, k to last 2 sts, turn to work RS.

Row 3 (RS): K to last st, sl1 wyif.
Row 4 (WS): Kfb, k to 2 sts before last turn, turn to work RS.

Repeat last 2 rows 46 more times. 108 sts.

Next Row (RS): K to last st, sl1 wyif.
Next Row (WS): K12, (yo, k2tog) 48 times.

Work a three-needle BO with these 108 sts together with the 108 sts from SECTION 10 brioche. This three-needle BO will join the 2 sections together.

Three Needle Bind Off: This bind off is worked looking at the wrong sides of the sections so the right sides of SECTION 12 and SECTION 10 should be facing each other like they are the inside of a sandwich. SECTION 12 sts should be on 1 needle and SECTION 10 sts should be on a separate needle.
Using a third needle, knit the first SECTION 12 stitch together with the first SECTION 10 stitch.
*Knit the next SECTION 12 stitch together with the next SECTION 10 stitch.
There should be 2 sts on your right needle.
Pass the first stitch over to bind off 1.
Repeat from * until all sts are bound off.

If this method is confusing to you, you can just bind off all SECTION 10 & 12 sts with a regular bind off and then seam the bound off edges together. The three-needle bind off is magical because you bind off both edges while "seaming" them together at the same time.

SECTION 13 - Garter Stitch Short Rows - Left Side

Color: I recommend doing a **Standard Marl** for this seed stitch section.

Row 1 (RS): Using 2 new strands of yarn, pick up and knit sts along the yarn over edge of SECTION 1 as follows, (pick up and k5, m1) 10 times. 60 sts. Turn to work WS.
Row 2 (WS): K to last st, sl1 wyif.

Row 3 (RS): Kfb, k to last 2 sts, turn to work WS.
Row 4 (WS): K to last st, sl1 wyif.

Row 5 (RS): Kfb, k to 2 sts before last turn, turn to work WS.
Row 6 (WS): K to last st, sl1 wyif.

Repeat last 2 rows 46 more times. 108 sts.

Next Row (RS): K12, (yo, k2tog) 48 times.

Work a three needle BO with these 108 sts together with the 108 sts from SECTION 5.

SECTION 14 - Garter Stich - Center Back

Color: I recommend doing a **Steady Marl** or **Fading Marl** for this back garter stitch section. I held 1 strand of gray mohair throughout the entire section and used about 5 speckled colors for my second strand.

Using 2 new strands of yarn, CO 32 sts. K32.

You will begin working back and forth while attaching your garter stitch panel to the selvedge sts from SECTION 9 & SECTION 3. As you attach these sections together, ignore the first 10 selvedge sts from SECTION 9 & SECTION 3. These will become part of the neckline later.

Row 1 (RS): Sl1 wyif, place yarn in back, k30, sl2 wyif (last stitch and a picked up selvedge stitch from SECTION 9).
Row 2 (WS): K2tog, k30, ssk (last stitch together with a picked up selvedge stitch from SECTION 3).

Repeat last 2 rows twice more.

Row 7 (RS): Sl1 wyif, place yarn in back, k30, sl1 wyif, turn to work WS.
Row 8 (WS): K2tog, k31, turn to work RS.

Repeat Rows 1-8 until all SECTION 3 & SECTION 9 selvedge sts should be joined together with this new garter stitch panel.

Next Row (RS): Sl1 wyif, place yarn in back, kfb, k to last st, sl2 wyif (last stitch and a picked up selvedge stitch from SECTION 10).
Next Row (WS): K2tog, kfb, k to last st, ssk (last stitch together with a picked up selvedge stitch from SECTION 5).

Repeat last 2 rows 37 more times. 108 sts. Break yarn.

FINISHING & EDGINGS

I-cord edging for sweater length: Choose 2 new colors for your I-cord edge around the bottom of the sweater. I held 1 DK weight together with 1 fingering weight yarn for a dense I-cord. You will need a long circular needle or you can distribute the sts onto 2 circular needles as you pick up and knit around the bottom perimeter. Continue with Bottom Edge Pick Up

Bottom edge pick up for longer dress length: Choose 2 colors held together to pick up sts and continue knitting a long dress in the round for the mesh and brioche border. I held 1 strand of mohair silk together with 1 strand of fingering weight speckled yarn.

BOTTOM EDGE PICK UP

K123 sts from SECTION 14 back garter stitch panel.
(Pick up and k3, m1) from SECTION 12 selvedge.
(Pick up and k3, m1) from SECTION 11 selvedge.
Pick up and k1 for each selvedge stitch from SECTION 6.
Pick up and k40 from SECTION 1 edge.
(Pick up and k3, m1) from SECTION 13 selvedge.

Continue with Sweater BO instructions or skip to Dress Version instructions.

Sweater I-cord BO: Cast on 3 sts using the cable cast on method and bind off all sts as follows, *k2, k2tog tbl, slip stitch onto left needle, repeat from * until all sts are bound off. Break yarn and pull it through the remaining 3 sts. Continue with Cuff and Collar instructions.

Dress Version

Place marker and join to work in the round. There should be an even number of sts. If you have an odd number of sts, decrease a stitch somewhere.

(YO, k2tog) to end of rnd.
K 1 rnd.

Repeat last 2 rnds until you are ready for the brioche border. Sample mesh measure 9" / 23cm.

I switched to a dark blue for my next 3 brioche rounds.

Brioche Rnd 1: (K1, sl1yo) to end of rnd.
Brioche Rnd 2: (Sl1yo, brp1) to end of rnd.

Brioche Rnd 3: (Brk1, sl1yo) to end of rnd.
Brioche Rnd 4: (Sl1yo, brp1) to end of rnd.

Repeat last 2 rnds until the brioche border reaches your desired length ending with Rnd 4. Sample measures 3" / 8cm. I used a fading marl to transition from light peach to a fiery saturated red-orange.

Next Rnd: (Brk1, k1) to end of rnd.

Choose 2 strands held together for your I-cord BO.

I-cord BO: Cast on 3 sts using the cable cast on method and bind off all sts as follows, *k2, k2tog tbl, slip stitch onto left needle, repeat from * until all sts are bound off. Break yarn and pull it through the remaining 3 sts.

Left Sleeve Cuff

Try using 1 needle size smaller for your cuffs and collar for a tight crisp look. I used one strand of DK weight held together with one strand of fingering weight for extra density. Two strands of fingering weight will also work.

Using 2 new strands of yarn and with RS facing, pick up and k40 sts along SECTION 5 selvedge.
(K2, p2) in the round until sleeve cuff reaches your desired length. Sample cuffs measure 6" / 15cm.

BO all sts using an I-cord BO.

Right Sleeve Cuff

Using 2 new strands of yarn and with RS facing, pick up and k40 sts along SECTION 10 selvedge.
(K2, p2) in the round until sleeve cuff reaches your desired length. BO all sts using an I-cord BO.

Using 2 new strands of yarn and with RS facing, pick up and k27 sts from back neck. There are 32 sts along the back neck edge, so skip 5 sts as you are picking them up to create a tidy and more tapered collar.
Pick up and k10 sts from SECTION 9 selvedge.
Pick up and k32 sts from SECTION 6 selvedge.
Pick up and k10 sts from SECTION 3 selvedge.
79 total sts.

Place marker and join to work in the rnd. K 16 rnds. BO all sts. Create a hem by folding the fabric in half and seaming the BO edge to inside edge of the collar (along the edge where you picked up sts).

Weave in ends. If you have long yarn tails from the two mesh sections, you can create decorative braids with those yarn ends instead of weaving them in.

Use this video from my Marled Magic Shawl to assist with weaving in your ends or braiding your ends.
https://youtu.be/fBshZjee_aA

SMALL SIZE DRESS VERSION
Knit by Linda Björk Eiríksdóttir

Modifications: Seed stitch and knit/purl rows around the bottom edge to achieve the dress length. Shorter cuff length.

PARACHUTEY

PARACHUTEY

Don't know what to do with all your fingering weight yarn leftovers? Knit a stripey tank top! The front is knit sideways with vertical garter stitch stripes. The back is worked from the neck down to the bottom while being attached to the front. The neckline and armholes are finished with crisp I-cord edges. The large voluminous shape is meant to have an oversized fit so you can move easily and breezily. Try cotton, silk, and linen yarns for warmer climates and layer Parachutey over t-shirts and long sleeves for a variety of styles.

Sizes: S [M, L, XL]

Finished Measurements: 55 [63, 72, 78]" / 140 [160, 183, 198]cm chest circumference. Large size shown on a 41" / 104cm chest circumference. Garment is designed to fit with generous positive ease.

Yarn: Fingering & lace weight

Yarn Amount: 200-300g of fingering and lace weight yarns. The large sample used approximately 240g of yarn.

Shown in: Primary Version (Large) - The Plucky Knitter Primo Fingering, A Verb for Keeping Warm Even Tinier Annapurna, Floating, & Kush, Madelinetosh Tosh Merino Light, Malabrigo Sock, Zen Yarn Garden Serenity 20, Elsa Wool Cormo Fingering, Bart & Francis Mohair/Silk Boucle (white lace weight mohair for the back section)

Purple & Neutral Version (Large) - Walk Collection Cottage Merino, Hedgehog Fibres Sock, Cashmere, & Kidsilk Lace, La Bien Aimée Merino Singles, Qing Fibre Mohair Silk

Needles: 40" US 4 / 3.5mm circular

Notions: Tapestry needle

Gauge: 20 sts & 52 rows = 4" / 10cm in garter stitch

Pattern Notes: Play with random striping sequences and enjoy mixing colors and fibers together. The primary color sample shows several fingering weight wools and sock yarns on the front. The back is mostly lace weight mohair boucle with fingering weight striped accents. The entire garment is knit in garter stitch, but feel free to substitute other stitch patterns like seed stitch or some decorative eyelet rows. The purple version is shown with seed stitch panels at the center front and there are a couple blocks of seed stitch on the back as well.

INSTRUCTIONS

LEFT FRONT
CO 2 sts.

Next Row (WS): Kfb, sl1 wyif.

Row 1 (RS): Kfb, k to last st, sl1 wyif.
Row 2 (WS): Kfb, k to last st, sl1 wyif.

Repeat last 2 rows 38 [48, 58, 68] more times. 81 [101, 121, 141] sts.

NECK SHAPING
Row 1 (RS): K to last st, sl1 wyif.
Row 2 (WS): K to last 3 sts, k2tog, sl1 wyif.

Repeat last 2 rows 19 more times. 61 [81, 101, 121] sts.

Next Row (RS): K to last st, sl1 wyif.
Next Row (WS): K to last st, sl1 wyif.

Repeat last 2 rows 14 [19, 29, 29] more times.

Next Row (RS): Kfb, k to last st , sl1 wyif.
Next Row (WS): K to last st, sl1 wyif.

Repeat last 2 rows 19 more times. 81 [101, 121, 141] sts.

RIGHT FRONT
Row 1 (RS): K to last st, sl1 wyif.
Row 2 (WS): K1, ssk, k to last 3 sts, k2tog, sl1 wyif.

Repeat last 2 rows until 5 sts remain.

Next Row (RS): K to last st, sl1 wyif.
Next Row (WS): K1, SK2P, sl1 wyif. 3 sts. Break yarn and pull strand through the 3 sts.

UPPER BACK
CO 45 [50, 60, 60] sts.

Next Row (WS): Kfb, k to last st, sl1 wyif.

Row 1 (RS): Kfb, k to last st, sl1 wyif.
Row 2 (WS): Kfb, k to last st, sl1 wyif.

Repeat last 2 rows 38 [48, 58, 68] more times. 124 [149, 179, 199] sts.

LOWER BACK
Row 1 (RS): CO 13 sts using the cable CO method, k to last st, CO 12 sts using the cable CO method, slip 1 selvedge st onto needle from bottom diagonal Right Front edge (next to CO).
Row 2 (WS): K2tog (first Back st together with picked up selvedge st), kfb, k to last st, ssk (last st together with a picked up selvedge st from bottom diagonal Left Front edge). 126 [151, 181, 201] sts.

Row 3 (RS): Sl1 wyif then place the yarn in back to knit, kfb, k to last st, sl2 wyif (last st & next selvedge st from bottom diagonal Right Front edge).
Row 4 (WS): K2tog (first Back st together with picked up selvedge st), kfb, k to last st, ssk (last st together with next selvedge st from bottom diagonal Left Front edge).

Repeat last 2 rows 38 [48, 58, 68] more times.

I-CORD EDGES
Using a contrast color, k all sts, pick up and k all sts along Front selvedge (1 st into each selvedge st). Work I-cord BO

I-cord BO: CO 3 sts using the cable CO method. *K2, k2tog tbl, place 3 sts back onto left needle, repeat from * until all sts are bound off. Break yarn and pull strand through the remaining 3 sts.

Using a contrast color, pick up and k1 st into each selvedge st along the Front neck edge. Turn to work WS. Work I-cord BO. Seam Front and Back shoulders together.

Using a contrast color, pick up and k1 st into each selvedge st around armhole. When you pick up sts along the increase or decrease diagonal edges, (pick up and k3, m1 using a backwards loop cast on) so the armhole edges are relaxed. Work I-cord BO. Repeat for the other armhole.

FINISHING

Weave in ends and block the finished tank top
to smooth the fabric. The purple version was
beaded along the neckline afterwards with a
variety of round beads.

PARACHUTEY DRESS

Size: Large

Finished Measurements:
40" / 102cm from shoulder to bottom edge, 72" / 183cm body circumference

Yarn: Fingering weight held double for a worsted weight gauge. You can substitute DK or Worsted weight yarn held single for this dress.

Yardage: Gather a big pile of scraps and single skeins and mix them all together. More is more and less is a bore!

Shown in: A collection of wool, cotton, silk, mohair, and linen yarns. Hold 2 strands together and change 1 strand of yarn at a time for a marled fade effect.

Needles: 40" US 8 / 5mm circular

Gauge: 18 sts & 32 rows = 4" / 10cm in garter stitch

Modifications: Thicker yarn and larger needle size. Extra garter stitch gussets at each side under the armhole. 2.5" / 6cm garter stitch border knit in the round along the bottom edge. Followed the Large size as written, but used the Medium size neck instructions.

PENGUONO

PENGUONO

Gather a colorful array of yarns from your collection and knit a dreamy convertible jacket! Begin with a seed stitch rectangle followed by a series of welts on the back. The sides and fronts are knit sideways in garter stitch with simple v-neck shaping. Then, work two rectangles for the shoulders and tapered seed stitch sleeves. Garter stitch short rows form the collar and another garter stitch rectangle forms the bottom band, all outlined in I-cord. Penguono is a fun short sleeved jacket during the day, but flip it upside down and it becomes a long dramatic coat for evening wear. I imagine if a Penguin were to wear a woolly kimono-esque jacket in my dream world, it would look something like this, a Penguono!

Sizes: S [M, L, XL, XXL, XXXL]
Shown in size XXL (purple/pink version) & XL (yellow sample & sample with pastel speckles/neon green sleeves).

Finished Measurements: 42 [48, 54, 60, 68, 80]" / 107 [122, 137, 152, 173, 203]cm chest circumference.
11 [12, 13.5, 15, 18, 22]" / 28 [31, 34, 38, 47, 56] cm armhole circumference

18 [19, 21, 24, 27, 31]" / 46 [48, 53, 61, 69, 79] cm long from top shoulder to bottom waist

Garment is designed to fit with a dramatically oversized, boxy effect.

Chest circumference is determined by row gauge so you can mix yarns with a different needle and gauge for another size.

Size	Chest circumference	4" / 10cm in garter stitch	Recommended yarn weight
S	42" / 107cm	20 sts / 44 rows	Fingering
M	48" / 122cm	18 sts / 40 rows	DK
L	54" / 137cm	16 sts / 36 rows	DK / Worsted
XL	60" / 152cm	14 sts / 32 rows	Worsted/Aran
XXL	68" / 173cm	12 sts / 28 rows	Chunky
XXXL	80" / 203cm	10 sts / 24 rows	Chunky

Yarn: Use stash and scrap yarns of all weights by holding them together to get your desired gauge. Have fun and play with different fibers and adventurous color combinations. The XXL sample pictured used the following yarns held together for a chunky weight gauge.

- 1 strand chunky weight
- 1 strand worsted weight + 1 strand fingering or lace weight
- 2 strands DK weight
- 3 strands fingering weight
- 1 strand DK weight + 2 strands fingering or lace weight

Yardage: Approximately 800 [900, 1000, 1100, 1200, 1300]g total

Needles: 40" US 10.5 / 6.5mm circular (for XXL size) or size needed to obtain gauge

Notions: 1 stitch marker, 1 split ring marker, tapestry needle

Gauge: 20 [18, 16, 14, 12, 10] sts & 44 [40, 36, 32, 28, 24] rows = 4" / 10cm in garter stitch

Pattern Notes: Instructions include when to break yarn after each section, but instructions do not indicate exactly what colors to use or when to stripe yarns. Those choices are totally up to you! Improvise and play with stripes and color blocks within each section.

The instructions include several photos to use for color and construction reference. As you knit each section, you can refer to this front and back view to visualize and plan your color choices. Each number corresponds to that section's number in the written instructions.

Choosing Yarns

Build your Penguono palette with a colorful array of fibers that inspire you. Focus on color and texture first. The yarn weight isn't as important because you can always hold two or three strands of yarn together to get a thicker gauge. A little bit of color can go a long way when you mix color pops with neutrals. Gather a range of light to dark colors to produce a variety of shadows and highlights throughout your project.

I recommend using several lofty wools like Shetland wool, Brooklyn Tweed SHELTER, and other woolen spun yarns to prevent your garment from becoming too heavy. Kidsilk mohair and thicker mohair boucle yarns help with color blending and they soften the overall feel of the fabric. If a color or texture doesn't seem to work, then just add ten more colors. Start with yarns from your curated collection and remember, when you use what you have, you deserve to buy more yarn!

INSTRUCTIONS

1. BACK

Provisionally CO 50 sts.

Next Row (WS): (K1, p1) to last 2 sts, k1, sl1 wyif.

Row 1 (RS): (K1, p1) to last 2 sts, k1, sl1 wyif.
Row 2 (WS): (K1, p1) to last 2 sts, k1, sl1 wyif.

Repeat last 2 rows 64 more times.

Next Row (RS): BO 12 sts, k26, place those 26 sts onto waste yarn, BO 12 sts. Break yarn.

2. LEFT WELTS

With RS facing, pick up and k66 sts along left selvedge. Start picking up sts at the corner by the 12 bound off shoulder sts.

*Next Row (WS): P all sts.

Row 1 (RS): K all sts.
Row 2 (WS): P all sts.

Repeat last 2 rows 3 more times.

Row 9 (RS): Using a new color, form a welt by knitting 1 live stitch together with 1 picked up stitch from 8 rows below. Follow the stitch column down 8 rows and pick up a purl bump on the WS of the work.

Repeat from * twice more. There should be 3 welts. Use a new color for each welt. Break yarn after last RS row. Slide sts to work another RS row for Row 1 of Left Back.

3. LEFT BACK

Row 1 (RS): Slip first 28 sts onto waste yarn, k37, sl1 wyif.
Row 2 (WS): K37, sl1 wyif.

Row 3 (RS): K37, sl1 wyif.
Row 4 (WS): K37, sl1 wyif.

Repeat last 2 rows 12 more times. Break yarn. Place 38 sts onto waste yarn.

4. RIGHT WELTS

With RS facing, pick up and k66 sts along right selvedge. Start picking up sts at the corner by the cast on edge.

Repeat from * 3 times (same as Left Welts). Break yarn after last RS row. Join yarn to work another RS row for Right Back Row 1.

5. RIGHT BACK

Row 1 (RS): K37, sl1 wyif, slip last 28 sts onto waste yarn.
Row 2 (WS): K37, sl1 wyif.

Row 3 (RS): K37, sl1 wyif.
Row 4 (WS): K37, sl1 wyif.

Repeat last 2 rows 12 more times. Break yarn.

6. RIGHT SIDE

Keep the 38 sts from Right Back on the needle. CO 10 sts.

Row 1 (RS): K9, sl2 wyif (last CO st together & first live st from Right Back).
Row 2 (WS): K2tog, k8, sl1 wyif.

Row 3 (RS): K9, sl2 wyif (10th st together with next live st from Right Back).
Row 4 (WS): K2tog, k8, sl1 wyif.

Repeat last 2 rows 36 more times. Break yarn, place 10 sts onto waste yarn.

7. RIGHT FRONT

WIth RS facing pick up and k38 sts along Right Side selvedge.

Next Row (WS): K37, sl1 wyif.

Row 1 (RS): K37, sl1 wyif.
Row 2 (WS): K37, sl1 wyif.

Repeat last 2 rows 12 more times.

Row 27 (RS): K38, CO 28 sts using the cable CO method. 66 sts.
Row 28 (WS): K65, sl1 wyif.

Row 29 (RS): K65, sl1 wyif.
Row 30 (WS): K65, sl1 wyif.

Repeat last 2 rows 16 more times.

Row 63 (RS): K to last st, sl1 wyif.
Row 64 (WS): K3, ssk, k to last st, sl1 wyif.

Repeat last 2 rows 34 more times. 31 sts.
Break yarn. Place 31 sts onto waste yarn.

8. LEFT SIDE

Place 38 sts from Left Back onto needle. The following rectangle is attached to the Left Back sts while it is being knit.
CO 10 sts.

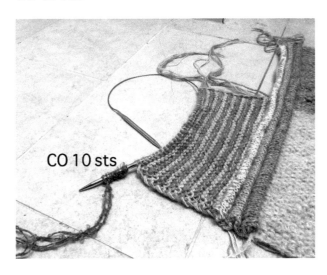

CO 10 sts

Next Row (WS): K9, ssk, (10th st together with Left Back st).

Row 1 (RS): Sl1 wyif, move yarn to back of work, k8, sl1 wyif.
Row 2 (WS): K9, ssk, (10th st together with next Left Back st).

Repeat last 2 rows 36 more times. Break yarn, place 10 sts onto waste yarn.

9. LEFT FRONT

With RS facing, pick up and k38 sts along Left Side selvedge.

Next Row (WS): K37, sl1 wyif.

Row 1 (RS): K37, sl1 wyif.
Row 2 (WS): K37, sl1 wyif.

Repeat last 2 rows 12 more times.

Row 27 (RS): CO 28 sts, k65, sl wyif. 66 sts.
Row 28 (WS): K65, sl1 wyif.

Row 29 (RS): K65, sl1 wyif.
Row 30 (WS): K65, sl1 wyif.

Repeat last 2 rows 16 more times.

Row 63 (RS): K to last st, sl1 wyif.
Row 64 (WS): K to last 5 sts, k2tog, k2, sl1 wyif.

Repeat last 2 rows 34 more times. 31 sts.
Break yarn. Place 31 sts onto waste yarn.

BACK, SIDE & FRONT SECTIONS

10. LEFT SHOULDER
CO 12 sts.

K 36 rows back and forth in garter stitch (18 garter ridges). Break yarn and leave sts on needle. The live sts should be by the armhole and the CO edge should be by the neck edge. Seam shoulder rectangle to Left Front and Left Back. When seaming shoulder to the back, seam 12 shoulder garter ridges to the 12 bound off back sts, then seam the remaining 6 shoulder garter ridges to the welt edge.

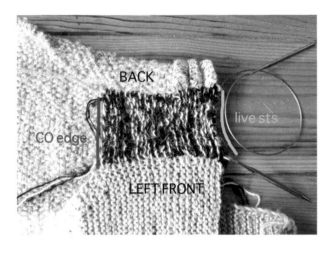

11. LEFT SLEEVE
With RS facing, pick up and k28 sts from Left Front, k12 shoulder sts, k28 sts from waste yarn (by the Left Welts). 68 sts. Turn to work WS row.

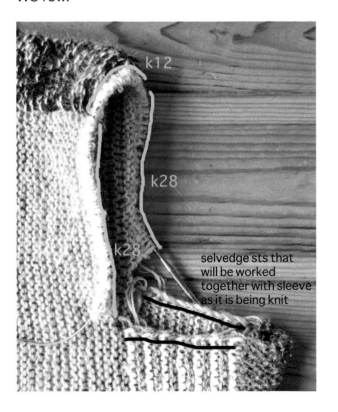

Next Row (WS): (K1, p1) to end of row.

The following rows form the seed stitch sleeve while it is being attached to the Left Back and Left Front selvedge sts.

Row 1 (RS): Sl1 wyif, move yarn to back of work, (k1, p1) to last st, sl1 wyif, sl1 selvedge st (from Left Back) wyif.

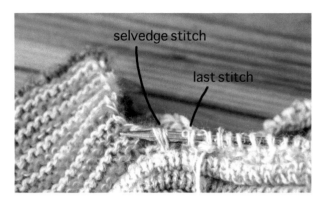

Row 2 (WS): K2tog, (p1, k1) to last st, ssk (last st together with a picked up selvedge st from Left Front).

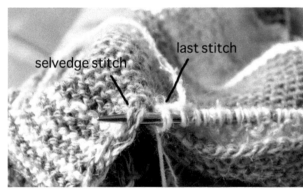

Row 3 (RS): Sl1 wyif, move yarn to back of work, (k1, p1) to last st, sl1 wyif, sl next selvedge st (from Left Back) wyif.
Row 4 (WS): K2tog, (p1, k1) to last st, ssk (last st together with the next picked up selvedge st from Left Front).

Repeat last 2 rows 12 more times. All 14 selvedge sts from Left Back and Left Front should be attached to the sleeve.

Row 29 (RS): K1, (k1, p1) to last st, sl1 wyif.
Row 30 (WS): K1, (p1, k1) to last st, sl1 wyif.

Repeat last 2 rows 3 more times.

Row 37 (RS): K2, k2tog, (p1, k1) to last 4 sts, p2tog, p1, sl1 wyif.
Row 38 (WS): K1, p2, (k1, p1) to last 3 sts, k2, sl1 wyif.
Row 39 (RS): K2, p2tog, (k1, p1) to last 4 sts, ssk, p1, sl1 wyif.
Row 40 (WS): (K1, p1) to last 2 sts, k1, sl1 wyif.

Repeat last 4 rows 5 more times. Break yarn, place remaining 44 sts onto waste yarn.

12. RIGHT SHOULDER
CO 12 sts.

K 36 rows back and forth in garter stitch (18 garter ridges). Break yarn and leave sts on needle. The live sts should be by the armhole and the CO edge should be by the neck edge. Seam shoulder rectangle to Right Front and Right Back. When seaming shoulder to the back, seam 12 shoulder garter ridges to the 12 bound off back sts, then seam the remaining 6 shoulder garter ridges to the welt edge.

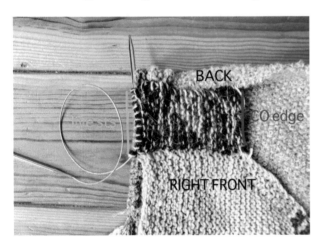

13. RIGHT SLEEVE
With RS facing, k28 sts from waste yarn (by the Right Welts), k12 shoulder sts, pick up and k28 sts from Right Front. 68 sts. Turn to work WS row.

Next Row (WS): (K1, p1) to end of row.

The following rows form the seed stitch sleeve while it is being attached to the Right Front and Right Back selvedge sts.

Row 1 (RS): Sl1 wyif, move yarn to back of work, (k1, p1) to last st, sl1 wyif, sl1 selvedge st (from Right Front) wyif.
Row 2 (WS): K2tog, (p1, k1) to last st, ssk (last st together with a picked up selvedge st from Right Back).

Row 3 (RS): Sl1 wyif, move yarn to back of work, (k1, p1) to last st, sl1 wyif, sl next selvedge st (from Right Front) wyif.
Row 4 (WS): K2tog, (p1, k1) to last st, ssk (last st together with the next picked up selvedge st from Right Back).

Repeat last 2 rows 12 more times. All 14 selvedge sts from Right Front and Right Back should be attached to the sleeve.

Work the rest of the sleeve using Left Sleeve instructions starting with Row 29 (RS).

14. UNDERARMS & SLEEVE CUFFS
Place 10 sts from Right Side onto needle.

Row 1 (RS): Sl1 wyif, move yarn to back of work, k8, sl1 wyif, sl next selvedge st (from Right Sleeve) wyif.

Row 2 (WS): K2tog, k8, ssk (last st together with the next picked up selvedge st from Right Sleeve).

Repeat last 2 rows 16 more times. Break yarn.

Using a contrasting color, k10, k44 sleeve sts. 54 sts. Place marker and join to work in the rnd.

P all sts.

K all sts.
P all sts.

Repeat last 2 rnds once more. BO all sts on the next rnd as follows, (k2tog tbl, place st back onto left needle) to end of rnd. Break yarn.

Repeat Underarm and Sleeve Cuff instructions for the Left Sleeve.

15. BORDER 1
Follow instructions for a garter stitch border or an optional two-color brioche border (shown on the pastel speckles/neon green sleeves sample)

GARTER STITCH VERSION
WIth RS facing, pick up and knit approximately 240 sts along bottom straight edge starting at the Left Front corner. Pick up and k1 into each selvedge st, pick up and k6 sts along each welt edge, pick up and k1 into each Back CO stitch.

Next Row (WS): K to last st, sl1 wyif.

Row 1 (RS): K to last st, sl1 wyif.
Row 2 (WS): K to last st, sl1 wyif.

Repeat last 2 rows 9 more times or until the border reaches your desired length. Break yarn and place sts onto a spare circular needle. Continue with Section 16. Border 2.

TWO-COLOR BRIOCHE VERSION
WIth RS facing and using MC (main color for the foreground), pick up and knit approximately 241 sts along bottom straight edge starting at the Left Front corner. Get these sts by picking up and knitting 1 st into each selvedge st, pick up and k6 sts along each welt edge, pick up and k1 into each Back CO stitch. You should have 241 total sts, but if you are missing a few sts or have a couple extra sts, that is fine as long as your total stitch count is uneven. Slide sts to work the same side with your CC (contrast color for the background).

Row 1 CC (RS): Using CC, sl1, p1, (sl1yo, p1) to last st, sl1 wyif.

Row 2 MC (WS): Using MC, k1, sl1yo, (brp1, sl1yo) to last st, sl1 wyif. Do not turn. Slide sts to work the WS with CC.

Row 2 CC (WS): Using CC, sl1 wyib, brk1, (sl1yo, brk1) to last st, sl1 wyib. Turn to work RS.

Row 3 MC (RS): Using MC, k1, sl1yo, (brk1, sl1yo) to last st, sl1 wyif.

Row 3 CC (WS): Using CC, sl1 wyif, brp1, (sl1yo, brp1) to last st, sl1 wyif.

Repeat Rows 2 & 3 using MC & CC 6 more times or until the border reaches your desired length ending with Row 2 CC (WS). Break CC.

Next Row MC (RS): Using MC, k2, (brk1, k1) to last st, sl1 wyif. Break yarn and place sts onto a spare circular needle.

16. BORDER 2

Pick up and k36 sts along Right Front selvedge (diagonal decrease edge), pick up and k12 sts along Right Shoulder, k26 Back sts, pick up and k12 sts along Left Shoulder, pick up and k36 sts along Left Front selvedge (diagonal decrease edge). 122 sts.

Next Row (WS): K to last st, sl1 wyif.

Row 1 (RS): K to last 3 sts, turn to work WS.

Row 2 (WS): K to last 3 sts, turn to work RS.

Row 3 (RS): K to 3 sts before last turn, turn to work WS.

Row 4 (WS): K to 3 sts before last turn, turn to work RS.

Repeat last 2 rows 9 more times.

Row 23 (RS): K to last st while closing the short row gaps, sl1 wyif.

Row 24 (WS): K to last st while closing the short row gaps, sl1 wyif.

Next Row (RS): Using contrasting yarn, k all BODER 2 sts, k31 sts from LEFT FRONT, pick up and k10 selvedge sts from BORDER 1, k all sts from BORDER 1, pick up and k10 selvedge sts from BORDER 1, k31 sts from RIGHT FRONT.

BO all sts using an I-cord BO as follows, CO 3 sts using the cable CO method, *k2, k2tog tbl, place 3 sts back onto left needle, repeat from * until all sts are bound off.

FINISHING

Weave in ends and block finished garment to smooth the fabric.

PENGUONO TEXTURIZED

This extra special Penguono was knit by Kellene Kaas Carpenter following the original Penguono instructions. She added super textural yarns and substituted other stitch patterns spontaneously throughout each section.

Size: XXL

Yarn: Chunky weight. Most yarns are wool or wool blends including some chunky yarns and thinner yarns held together to achieve a chunky thickness. There are novelty yarns including sparkly sequins and mohair yarns held throughout some of the sections.

Needles: US 10.5 / 6.5mm circular

Modifications: Started with seed stitch for the back and then added other stitch patterns like loops, cables, and ribbing until the back reached the recommended row count. This first back piece is a large rectangle so you can use it as a landscaper for experimenting with colors and textures.

The sides and front feature extra knit/purl stitch patterns and fluffy textured yarns. Follow the stitch and row counts, but feel free to modify the simple stitch patterns and add your own personality to the fabric.

The sleeves blossom outward due to the dense chunky weight wool. The sleeves are knit from the shoulder to the cuff so you can make them as long as you want. The sample sleeves are tapered due to thinner worsted weight yarns and a smaller needle size. You can gradually decrease under the arm to taper the sleeves. Add welts or textured yarns to the sleeves to make them extra special.

PENGUONO MAXIMIZED

I created this ginormous Penguono using chunky yarns for a massive oversized coat. This XXXL size eats up a lot of yarn, but it's super cozy to the max!

Size: XXXL

Yarn: Chunky weight wools including Hedgehog Fibres Chubby and Malabrigo Chunky. I used lots of textured yarns like angora, brushed alpaca, and mohair.

Needles: US 13 / 9mm circular

ASKEWS ME
SWEATER
& DRESS

ASKEWS ME SWEATER & DRESS

Gather a selection of worsted and DK weight yarns for this top down brioche garment. The neck features a biased section that continues into the spiraling yoke. A single increase continues into the sweater body for a flared asymmetrical shape. The sample shows a consistent background color with stripes and color blocks in the foreground. Mix your collection of DK and worsted weight yarns together and also try holding fingering weight yarns double for a bright accent color. Try on the top down construction as you knit to get the perfect sleeve and body length.

Sizes: S [M, L, XL, XXL, XXL]
Sample shown in size XL on a 41" / 104cm chest circumference.

Finished Measurements: 41 [43, 46, 48, 50, 53]" / 104 [109, 117, 122, 127, 135]cm chest circumference. Sleeve length and body length are customizable.

Yarn: DK & Worsted weight

Yardage: Sweater requires approximately 1400 [1500, 1600, 1700, 1800, 1900]yds / 1280 [1372, 1463, 1554, 1646, 1737]m total
Dress requires approximately 1650 [1750, 1850, 1950, 2050, 2150]yds / 1509 [1600, 1692, 1783, 1875, 1966]m total

Shown in: Sweater Color A Foreground - Brooklyn Tweed SHELTER, Shibui Alpaca DK, Madelinetosh Tosh DK, Quince & Co. Owl Sweater Color B Background - Malabrigo Rios (black)

Dress Color A Foreground - Madelinetosh Tosh Merino DK & Tosh DK, Hedgehog Fibres Sock Yarn (held double), Lorna's Laces Masham Worsted, Blue Sky Alpacas Brushed Suri, Walk Collection Baby Blue Aran
Dress Color B Background - Quince & Co Owl (white) along with a couple other white yarns

Needles: 40" US 9 / 5.5mm circular
Magic loop method is used for knitting the neck and sleeves in the round.

Notions: 3 stitch markers, tapestry needle

Gauge: 14 sts & 20 rounds = 4" / 10cm in two-color brioche stitch (measured unstretched)

Pattern Notes: Instructions are written using color A and color B. Color A is the foreground color and color B is the background color. The samples show a consistent color B background color while color A changes in the foreground with color blocks and stripes. Feel free to change colors whenever you like. Changing both colors A & B will create a more striped graphic fabric. Keeping one of the colors consistent will ground the fabric and give it an overall quality of lightness or darkness. Experiment and play with colors and fibers to maintain your interest while knitting this garment.

INSTRUCTIONS

NECK

CO 84 sts loosely (with loose tension or with a needle that is a few sizes larger than the main needle) using the Two-Color CO.

TWO-COLOR CO

Tie both yarns together - remove the knot after working a few rows. Tie a slip knot in Color B and slide the slip knot onto the left-hand needle.

Step 1: Knit into the color B slip knot with color A, leaving the stitch on the left needle. Place the new stitch onto left needle, by slipping it knit-wise.
Step 2: Bring color B from behind and knit into gap between last two stitches on left needle with color B (like a cable CO).
Step 3: Place new knitted stitch onto left needle by slipping it knit-wise. Repeat Step 2 & 3 using color A. Continue casting on alternating color B & A until 84 sts are cast on.

Set Up Row 1A: Using A, (k1, sl1yo) to end of row. Slide sts to work the same side with color B.
Set Up Row 1B: Using B, (sl1yo, brp1) to end of row.

Place marker and join to work in the rnd.

Rnd 2A: Using color A, (brk1, sl1yo) to end of rnd.
Rnd 2B: Using color B, (sl1yo, brp1) to end of rnd.
Rnd 3A: Using color A, brkyobrk, sl1yo, (brk1, sl1yo) 12 times, brRsl dec, sl1yo, (brk1, sl1yo) to end of rnd.
Rnd 3B: Using color B, (sl1yo, brp1) to end of rnd.

Repeat Rnds 2 & 3 until work measures approximately 10" / 25cm ending with Rnd 2 using color B.

YOKE

Rnd 1A: Using color A, brkyobrk, sl1yo, *(brk1, sl1yo) 13 times, pm, brkyobrk, sl1yo, repeat from * once more, (brk1, sl1yo) 13 times. 6 sts increased.
Rnd 1B: Using color B, (sl1yo, brp1) to end of rnd.

Rnd 2A: Using color A, (brk1, sl1yo) to end of rnd.
Rnd 2B: Using color B, (sl1yo, brp1) to end of rnd.
Rnd 3A: Using color A, brkyobrk, sl1yo, *(brk1, sl1yo) to m, slm, brkyobrk, sl1yo, repeat from * once more, (brk1, sl1yo) to end of rnd. 6 sts increased.
Rnd 3B: Using color B, (sl1yo, brp1) to end of rnd.

Repeat Rnds 2 & 3 14 [16, 18, 20, 22, 24] more times, then Repeat Rnd 2 once more ending with Rnd 2 using color B. You should be able to count 32 [36, 40, 44, 48, 52] knit column sts from the Yoke. 180 [192, 204, 216, 228, 240] sts.

Next Rnd: Using color A, brkyobrk, sl1yo, *(brk1, sl1yo) 14 [15, 16, 17, 18, 19] times, slip next 30 [32, 34, 36, 38, 40] sts onto waste yarn for left sleeve, CO 12 sts using the cable CO method, remove marker, (brk1, sl1yo) 30 [32, 34, 36, 38, 40] times, remove marker, slip next 30 [32, 34, 36, 38, 40] sts onto waste yarn for right sleeve, CO 12 sts using the cable CO method, (brk1, sl1yo) 15 [16, 17, 18, 19, 20] times. 144 [152, 160, 168, 176, 184]
Next Rnd: Using color B, (sl1yo, brp1) 16 [17, 18, 19, 20, 21] times, (sl1yo, p1) 6 times, (sl1yo, brp1) 30 [32, 34, 36, 38, 40] times, (sl1yo, p1) 6 times, (sl1yo, brp1) 15 [16, 17, 18, 19, 20] times.

BODY

Rnd 1A: Using color A, (brk1, sl1yo) to end of rnd.

Rnd 1B: Using color B, (sl1yo, brp1) to end of rnd.

Rnd 2A: Using color A, brkyobrk, sl1yo, (brk1, sl1yo) to end of rnd. 2 sts increased.

Rnd 2B: Using color B, (sl1yo, brp1) to end of rnd.

Repeat Rnds 1 & 2 until work measures approximately 29" / 74cm (measure along back side without increases) from underarm ending with a color A rnd. Try on the garment as you reach the bottom edge so it is the length you want.

Next Rnd: Using color B or a contrast color of choice, (k1, brk1) to end of rnd.

BO all sts on the next rnd using an I-cord BO as follows, CO 3 sts using the cable CO method, *k2, k2tog tbl, slip 3 sts onto left needle, repeat from * until all sts are bound off. Break yarn and pull it through the remaining 3 sts.

LEFT SLEEVE

Place 30 [32, 34, 36, 38, 40] sleeve sts from waste yarn onto needle.

Set Up Row (RS): Using color A, (brk1, sl1yo) to end of row, pick up and k12 sts from underarm. 42 [44, 46, 48, 50, 52] sts.

Next Row (RS): Using color B, (sl1yo, brp1) to last 12 sts, (sl1yo, p1) 6 times. Skip to Both Sleeves Instructions.

RIGHT SLEEVE

Set Up Row (RS): Using color A, pick up and k12 sts from underarm, (brk1, sl1yo) to end of row. 42 [44, 46, 48, 50, 52] sts.

Next Row (RS): Using color B, (sl1yo, p1) 6 times, (sl1yo, brp1) to end of row.

BOTH SLEEVES

Place marker and join to work in the rnd.

Rnd 1A: Using color A, (brk1, sl1yo) to end of rnd.

Rnd 1B: Using color B, (sl1yo, brp1) to end of rnd.

For short sleeves like the dress version, repeat Rnd 1 Using A & B until sleeves reach desired length. Skip to I-cord BO.

For longer tapered sweater sleeves, repeat Rnd 1 Using A & B while working occasional Decrease Rnds. Determine approximately how long you want your sleeve to measure and how small you want the final circumference. Work a decrease rnd evenly throughout the sleeve until you reach your finished length.

Decrease Rnd (Left Sleeve Only): Using color A, (brk1, sl1yo) to last 4 sts, brRsl dec, sl1yo. 2 sts decreased.

Next Rnd: Using color B, (sl1yo, brp1) to end of rnd.

Decrease Rnd (Right Sleeve Only): Using color A, brLsl dec, sl1 yo, (brk1, sl1yo) to end of rnd. 2 sts decreased.

Next Rnd: Using color B, (sl1yo, brp1) to end of rnd.

Continue Repeating Rnd 1 Using A & B with the Decrease Rnd until sleeve reaches desired length ending with Rnd 1 Using color A. Break color A. Try on the sweater as you knit to customize the sleeve circumference and length.

Next Rnd: Using color B, (k1, brk1) to end of rnd.

I-cord BO: CO 3 sts using the cable CO method, *k2, k2tog tbl, slip 3 sts onto left needle, repeat from * until all stitches are bound off. Break yarn and pull strand through the remaining 3 sts.

FINISHING

Weave in ends and block or steam the garment to relax the fabric.

ASKEWS ME
DICKEY
& PONCHO

ASKEWS ME DICKEY & PONCHO

This two-color brioche accessory is the coziest layer with sweaters and jackets!
The top-down journey begins with a luscious turtleneck for ultra warmth.
An increase and decrease form a biased section that folds down for a stylish asymmetrical detail. Three increases produce the spiraling flared yoke.
The yoke length is customizable so you can bind off for a dickey or continue increasing for a large poncho.

Sizes: Dickey [Poncho]

Finished Measurements: 20" / 51cm neck circumference, 8" / 20cm neck length, 6 [17]" / 15 [43]cm yoke length (customizable)

Yarn: DK weight

Yardage: Color A - 220 [630]yds / 201 [576]m
Color B - 200 [600]yds / 183 [549]m

Shown in: Poncho - Woolfolk FÅR
(100% Merino Wool; 142yds / 130m per 50g skein)
Color A - 05 Black, Color B - 01 White

Dickey - Woolfolk FÅR
Color A - 01 White (foreground color)
Daruma Genmou (100% Merino Wool; 165yds / 151m per 50g ball)
Color B - 15 Green (background color)

Needles: 40" US 7 / 4.5mm circular
Magic loop method is used for knitting in the round.

Notions: 3 stitch markers, tapestry needle

Gauge: 16 sts & 26 rounds = 4" / 10cm in two-color brioche stitch (measured unstretched)

INSTRUCTIONS

NECK

Using A, CO 3 sts using an I-cord cast on. *Slip 3 sts to left needle, k3, repeat from * 83 more times. Slip 3 sts onto left needle, k3tog.

Pick up and k83 sts from I-cord edge. Slide sts to work the same side with color B.

Set Up Row 1: Using B, (sl1yo, brp1) to end of row.

Place marker and join to work in the round.

Rnd 2: Using A, (brk1, sl1yo) to end of rnd.
Rnd 2: Using B, (sl1yo, brp1) to end of rnd.
Rnd 3: Using A, brkyobrk, sl1yo, (brk1, sl1yo) 12 times, brRsl dec, sl1yo, (brk1, sl1yo) to end of rnd.
Rnd 3: Using B, (sl1yo, brp1) to end of rnd.

Repeat Rnds 2 & 3 25 more times or until work measures approximately 8" / 25cm (measured along vertical columns without shaping) ending with Rnd 2 using color B.

YOKE

Rnd 1: Using A, brkyobrk, sl1yo, *(brk1, sl1yo) 13 times, pm, brkyobrk, sl1yo, repeat from * once more, (bk1, sl1yo) 13 times. 6 sts increased.
Rnd 1: Using B, (sl1yo, brp1) to end of rnd.

Rnd 2: Using A, (brk1, sl1yo) to end of rnd.
Rnd 2: Using B, (sl1yo, brp1) to end of rnd.
Rnd 3: Using A, brkyobrk, sl1yo, *(brk1, sl1yo) to m, slm, brkyobrk, sl1yo, repeat from * once more, (brk1, sl1yo) to end of rnd. 6 sts increased.
Rnd 3: Using B, (sl1yo, brp1) to end of rnd.

Repeat Rnds 2 & 3 14 [50] more times or until work measures 6 [17]" / 15 [43]cm from beginning of Yoke or until the fabric reaches your desired length. Then, Repeat Rnd 2 once more ending with Rnd 2 using color B. Break color B.

Next Rnd: Using A, (brk1, k1) to end of rnd

I-cord BO: CO 3 sts using the cable CO method, *k2, k2tog tbl, slip 3 sts onto left needle, repeat from * until all stitches are bound off. Break yarn and pull strand through the remaining 3 sts.

FINISHING

Weave in ends and lightly block or steam the fabric.

Askews Me Poncho
Yarn: Woolfolk Får in color 12
Madelinetosh Tosh DK in Neon Peach

WATCH YOUR BACK

WATCH YOUR BACK

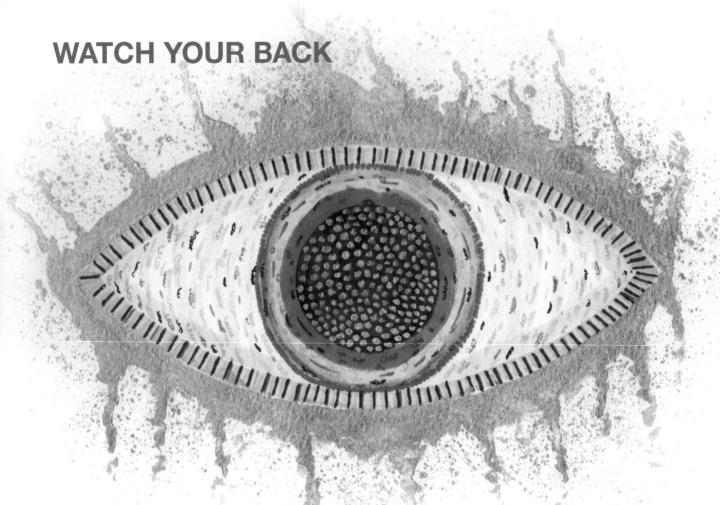

Create the knitted eyeball of your dreams with this cleverly constructed pattern. Start at the center and increase to form a circle for the pupil and iris. The white sections are knit back and forth in garter stitch with a brioche border framing the final shape. Use worsted weight yarns or hold two strands of fingering weight yarn together to get gauge. The samples use several fluffy textured yarns for a funky fuzzy eye. Drape the eyeball over your shoulders and fold over the top for a shawl collar or wrap it around like a cozy shawl.

Sizes: Small [Large]

Finished Measurements: 61 [84]" / 155 [213] cm long, 27 [32]" / 69 [81]cm wide.

Yarn: Worsted weight

Yardage: Color A - 250 [300]yds / 229 [274]m
Color B - 250 [300]yds / 229 [274]m
Color C - 600 [700]yds / 549 [640]m

Shown in: Color A (pupil & border)- Black cotton with gold metallic
Color B (iris) - Various fluffy novelty yarns and merino DK wools shown in blue and pink
Color C (sclera & border) - Sock yarn held double (shown in white/cream bases with bright speckles)

Needles: 47" or longer US 8 / 5mm circular. Use Magic loop method for knitting in the round until there are enough stitches to fit onto the circular needle.

Notions: 4 stitch markers, tapestry needle

Gauge: 18 sts & 34 rows = 4" / 10cm in garter stitch

INSTRUCTIONS

Using color A and Emily Ocker's circular cast on method, CO 8 sts. Place marker and join to work in the rnd.

m1: (make 1) increase 1 stitch by knitting into the back of the stitch in the row below.
In Rnd 1, m1 using the backwards loop CO method since this is the first rnd.

SECTION 1
Rnd 1: (K1, m1) 8 times. 16 sts.
Rnd 2: K16
Rnd 3: (K1, m1) 16 times. 32 sts.
Next 4 rnds: K32.
Rnd 8: (K1, m1) 32 times. 64 sts.
Next 7 rnds: K64.
Rnd 16: (K2, m1) 32 times. 96 sts.
Next 7 rnds: K96.

Continue by following Small or Large Size instructions.

Small Size Only
Break color A.

Rnd 24: Using B, (k2, m1) 48 times. 144 sts.
Next 11 Rnds: K144.
Rnd 36: (K2, m1) 72 times. 216 sts.
Next 19 rnds: K216.

Break color B.

Large Size Only
Rnd 24: (K2, m1) 48 times. 144 sts.
Next 11 Rnds: K144.

Break color A.

Rnd 36: Using color B, (k2, m1) 72 times. 216 sts.
Next 19 rnds: K216.
Rnd 56: (K3, m1) 72 times. 288 sts.
Next 19 rnds: K288.

Break color B.

SECTION 2
Row 1 (RS): Slip 53 [71] color B sts onto right needle. Using C, k3, turn to work WS.
Row 2 (WS): K3, turn to work RS.

These 2 photos demonstrate the color B pickup in Row 3…

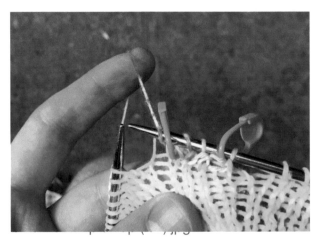

Row 3 (RS): Sl1 color B st onto left needle, k1, pm, k3, pm, k next color B st, turn to work WS.
Row 4 (WS): K5, turn to work RS.

Row 5 (RS): Sl1 color B st onto left needle, k to m, M1R, slm, k3, slm, M1L, k all color C sts, k next color B st.
Row 6 (WS): K all color C sts, turn to work RS.

Repeat last 2 rows 38 [56] more times. Break color C.

Next Row (RS): Sl13 color B sts from right needle onto left needle. Using a new strand of color C, k to m, M1R, slm, k3, slm, M1L, k all color C sts, k12 color B sts. Turn to work WS.

Next Row (WS): K all color C sts. Break color C.

There should be 188 [260] color C sts.

Leave all color C sts on the needle and repeat SECTION 2 with the other half of the color B sts.

Once both halves of SECTION 2 are complete there should be 376 [520] total color C sts.

SECTION 3 - Brioche Border
You will now knit all the way around the perimeter of the eye with color A starting at the stitch where you just broke color C.

Rnd 1: Using A, *(k1, sl1yo) to 1 st before m, k1, slm, sl1yo, k1, sl1yo, slm*, repeat from * to * once more, (k1, sl1yo) to last 3 sts, k2tog, sl1yo. Place marker to mark beginning of rnd.
Rnd 1: Using C, *(sl1yo, brp1) to 1 st before m, sl1yo, slm, brp1, slm, repeat from * once more, (sl1yo, brp1) to end of rnd.

Rnd 2: Using A, *(brk1, sl1yo) to 1 st before m, brkyobrk, slm, sl1yo, slm, brkyobrk, sl1yo, repeat from * once more, (brk1, sl1yo) to end of rnd.

Rnd 2: Using C, *(sl1yo, brp1) to 1 st before m, sl1yo, slm, brp1, slm, repeat from * once more, (sl1yo, brp1) to end of rnd.

Rnd 3: Using A, *(brk1, sl1yo) to 1 st before m, brk1, slm, sl1yo, slm, repeat from * once more, (brk1, sl1yo) to end of rnd.
Rnd 3: Using C, *(sl1yo, brp1) to 1 st before m, sl1yo, slm, brp1, slm, repeat from * once more, (sl1yo, brp1) to end of rnd.

Repeat Rnds 2 & 3 five more times. You should be able to count 13 total color A knit stitches in each vertical column. Break color C.

Next Rnd: Using A, *(brk1, k1) to 1 st before m, brk1, slm, k1, slm, repeat from * once more, (brk1, k1) to end of rnd.

FINISHING
Turn to I-cord BO on the WS. Using A, cast on 3 sts using the cable cast on method, *k2, k2tog tbl, sl3 sts onto left needle, repeat from * until all sts are bound off. Break yarn, weave in ends, and block the finished eye.

ABBREVIATIONS

BO: bind off

CO: cast on

k: knit

k2tog: knit 2 together

k3tog: knit 3 together

kfb: knit into front and back of stitch

m: marker

m1: (make 1) Increase 1 stitch using the backwards loop cast on method unless instructed otherwise.

M1L: (make 1 left) With left needle, lift strand between sts from the front, knit through the back loop.

M1R: (make 1 right) With left needle, lift strand between sts from the back, knit through the front loop.

p: purl

pm: place marker

rnd/s: round/s

RS: right side

sk2p: slip 1, knit 2 together, pass slipped stitch over

sl: slip (Slipped sts are slipped purl-wise unless instructed otherwise.)

slm: slip marker

ssk: slip slip knit

st/s: stitch/es

tbl: through back loop

WS: wrong side

wyif: with yarn in front

yf: yarn forward

yo: yarn over

Brioche Abbreviations

brk: brioche knit also known as bark, knit the stitch (that was slipped in the previous row) together with its yarn over.

brkyobrk: two stitches spring out of the center of one stitch with this increase. Work a brkyobrk as follows: brk1, yo (yarn forward under needle then over needle to back), then brk1 into same stitch. 2 sts increased.

brp: brioche purl also known as burp, purl the stitch (that was slipped in the previous row) together with its yarn over.

brLsl dec: (2-stitch decrease that slants to the left, involving 3 sts) slip the first stitch knit-wise, brk the following two stitches together, pass the slipped stitch over.

brRsl dec: (a 2-stitch decrease that slants to the right, involving 3 sts) slip the first stitch knitwise, knit the next stitch, pass the slipped stitch over, place stitch on left hand needle and pass the following stitch over. Place stitch on right hand needle.

sl1yo following a k or brk st: (slip 1 yarn over) bring the working yarn under the needle to the front of the work, slip the next stitch purl-wise, then bring the yarn over the needle (and over the slipped stitch) to the back, in position to work the following stitch.

sl1yo following a p or brp st: (slip 1 yarn over) working yarn is already in front, slip the next stitch purl-wise, then bring the yarn over the needle (and over the slipped stitch), then to the front under the needle, into position to work the following stitch.

In two-color brioche stitch, two rounds/rows are worked for each counted round/row that appears on the face of the fabric. The first color is worked around/across once and then the round/row is worked again using the second color. The next round/row is worked the same way, once around/across with the first color and worked again with the second color. When counting rounds/rows, count only the stitches going up on the knit column. For example, when you work 4 rounds/rows, count 4 knit column stitches, even though you will have worked 8 rounds/rows (4 with each color). 2 worked rounds/rows = 1 counted round/row.

When you put down your knitting and forget which color you just used and which color to use next, look at the color of the yo in the row just worked. That is the last color you used so it's time to work the next color.

I highly recommend Nancy Marchant's classes and books on brioche knitting especially her book Knitting Fresh Brioche, a comprehensive reference book filled with technique, stitch patterns, and designs.

www.briochestitch.com

PHOTO CREDITS

Photography by Jarrod Duncan & Grace DuVal

Parachutey Dress & Kangarorts (black sample) photos by Darren Smith

Askews Me Sweater & Dress and Parachutey studio photos & makeup
by Alexandra Feo

Burgundy/Peach Askews Me Poncho Photo by Jonna Jolkin

Necklaces, hats, & earrings handmade by Bitsch Kitsch in London.
Bitsch Kitsch styling selection by Dr. Manrutt Wongkaew

Styling: Stephen West

Styling assistance: Jessica Jeanne Eaton

Illustrations by Alexandra Dögg Steinþórsdóttir

SAMPLE KNITTERS

Linda Björk Eiríksdóttir - Enchanted Mesa Dress, Marled Magic Dress (green), Parachutey with beads

Kolbrún Jónsdóttir - Enchanted Mesa Sweater (black & blue sample)

Chantal Belisle - Kangarullover (speckled sample), Penguono (yellow sample)

Hólmfrídur Sverrisdóttir - Watch Your Back (small sample)

Beata Jezek - Penguono (purple/pink sample)

Kellene Kaas Carpenter - Penguono Texturized

Stephen West - all other samples

MODELS

Chantal Belisle, Linda Björk Eiríksdóttir, Alexandra Dögg Steinþórsdóttir, Karítas Árný Sturludóttir, Stephen West

Thank you Malia, Lou, and Nancy for your constant support and friendship.

CONTACT INFORMATION

Stephen West
www.westknits.com
www.stephenandpenelope.com

Customer support: support@westknits.com

r westknits

f www.facebook.com/westknits

[◉] www.instagram.com/westknits